Working V

Pacific Institute for Alexander Technique
930 Alhambra Blvd. #270
Sacramento, CA 95816
(916) 448-7424 • alextech@sirius.com

Working Without Pain

Eliminate Repetitive Strain Injuries
With the Alexander Technique

Sherry Berjeron-Oliver
& Bruce Oliver

Alexander Technique

Pacific Institute for
the Alexander Technique
Chico, California

Working Without Pain:
Eliminate Repetitive Strain Injuries
with Alexander Technique

Published by
The Pacific Institute for the Alexander Technique
1530 Humboldt, #4
Chico, CA 95928
(916) 895-3347
E-mail: piat@sunset.net

CATALOGING IN PUBLICATION DATA
Berjeron-Oliver, Sherry
Working without pain : eliminate repetitive strain injuries with
Alexander technique / Sherry Berjeron-Oliver & Bruce Oliver.

p.   cm.
Preassigned LCCN: 96-68768
ISBN 0-9651047-0-2
1. Overuse injuries—Treatment.   2. Alexander technique.
I. Oliver, Bruce.   II. Title

RD97.6.B47 1997   617.4'7044
                          QBI96-40284

ACKNOWLEDGEMENTS
Shoshana Alexander who made the book what it is today, Heidi Pfankuch for her continous friendship, Aldrich Patterson for planting the first seed, Cathy Pollock for helping to water the little sprouts and Gayle Kimball for her continual feedback. Jan Manella, Harriet Berman, Frances Schmookler and Naomi Davis for editting support. Peggy Stith and Marisol Mayell for their photographic assistance and all our trainees for the past 4 years. To my sister Alyson for being a great sister and Jeanne and Matt for their loving support.

Forward by Mayama Morehart, M.D.
Edited by Shoshana Alexander
Formatting by David Hurst
Cover design by Paul Bohanna
Cover photograph by John Shern
Illustrations by Catherine R. Seymour
Photography by Rudy Giscombe
Photograph model Dorothy Ormes

This book is dedicated to
Our children Cole and Alexandra for their patience
Our parents Harriet and Hack for their constant support
with love and gratitude

Contents

Foreword

As a clinical physician, I frequently see people whose true problem is body misuse rather than body malfunction. Carpel tunnel syndrome, thoracic outlet syndrome, tension neck, tendinitis, and back pain are often Repetitive Strain Injuries (RSI's) that are preventable by conscious and proper use of body mechanics. People in the modern workplace desperately need to regain awareness of how to consciously use their bodies.

Increased stimulation and overwhelming demands in the workplace require each of us to identify how we can inhibit harmful responses to outside stimuli. The Alexander Technique described by Sherry Berjeron-Oliver and Bruce Oliver in this book supports us in "reprogramming" inappropriate and unnecessary patterns of body movement, such as excessive muscular effort, that contribute to RSI's.

From my observation of others, I know that it is possible through the Alexander system to learn to control physical and emotional responses to outside stimuli. Since beginning Alexander lessons myself, I have personally experienced the benefits of this technique —increased poise and confidence, relief from and prevention of back pain, and loss of my life long speech impediment. The changes I have witnessed in myself and others have been beneficial and empowering.

~MAYAMA MOREHART, M.D.

Introduction

This book was conceived when we were listening to a program on National Public Radio about a pending lawsuit against the biggest computer companies in the world. The plaintiffs were attributing their various disabilities, such as carpal tunnel syndrome, to the design of computer keyboards. By that point, as teachers of the Alexander Technique, we had helped hundreds of people, from corporate offices to the medical establishment, who had similar problems to those on the radio program. We knew that while keyboard design does have some effect on the development of Repetitive Strain Injury (RSI), it is certainly not the root cause. Our clients had recovered from their injuries without surgery and gone on to use the same computer or instruments without future problems. Wanting to shed light on this commonly misunderstood problem, we decided to write a book for those who are at risk in the workplace.

There are numerous new and innovative approaches designed to stop and prevent the problem of Repetitive Strain Injuries. Furniture design, work scheduling, and equipment design hold some promise for reducing the problem. But external adjustments such as these are only part of the solution. That is because the core of the problem is how people use their bodies in response to circumstances at work.

The Alexander Technique has a 100 year history of success in helping people, such as musicians, writers and teachers rid themselves of RSI's. These same principles can be applied with great success to the problems developed in today's stressful workplace. However, simply telling people how to move correctly is for the most part unproductive for long term improvement. You may see pictures of correct postures or positions, but how do you get from where you are now to where you can automatically move safely with comfort and ease? Our belief is that the Alexander Technique student needs to make the same discoveries that F.M. Alexander himself made. That process is the basis of this book. Alexander was a Shakespearean actor who lived in Australia during the latter half of the nineteenth century. His career was jeopardized when his voice began to fail during performances. He worked with different doctors, specialists and teachers to solve his problem, none of which worked, before striking out on his own to discover what he was doing that was causing the loss of voice. Determined to get to the root cause, he began studying and experimenting with the postural arrangement of his whole body. He discovered that the way in which he balanced his head, neck and spine affected his entire physical and mental functioning. From that discovery, Alexander went on to scientifically test theories and develop principles that, as he applied them, led to his returning to the stage without his long standing voice problem. These principles and discoveries integrated into a method (or process) that is known today as the Alexander Technique. The information in this book can help you to start discovering the causes of RSI in yourself and to begin to grasp the principles that will lead you to prevention and recovery. In order to get the full benefit of the Alexander Technique, the guidance of a qualified teacher is invaluable. Yet even the best teachers in the world cannot help those who are unwilling to venture into change. Change begins with asking yourself, "What am I doing that is causing my injury or problem?"

Most of this book is designed to help you in examining this question and introducing the principles that can facilitate change in your work situation. The stories included throughout—drawn from our work with clients—are intended to help you see how other people have gotten help for Repetitive Strain Injuries with Alexander Technique. The guided procedures, in the book are gentle movements used to develop heightened awareness and specific skills unique to the Alexander Technique. Some of the procedures are routinely used by Alexander Technique teachers. Others are our adaptations of the skills and principles of the Alexander Technique specifically for use in the workplace.

All those in this book who successfully recovered from Repetitive Strain Injuries had the benefit of our hands-on guidance. While we would urge you to seek the assistance of a qualified Alexander Technique teacher, learning what is offered in this book with a calm, patient and repetitive approach, you can begin to discover the causes of RSI in yourself and to grasp the principles that will lead you to prevention and recovery. With no pre-defined principles or hands-on guidance, F.M. Alexander accomplished successful recovery from his problem. You, on the other hand, have the benefit of his discoveries by observing how they helped others. As you develop the skills offered in Working Without Pain, you may find that people will ask things like, Have you lost weight? Did you just go on a vacation? Our clients report that is not uncommon for others to ask if they have grown taller!

One of our students, Roger, came to us with chronic pain in his knees, lower back and shoulder that had grown continually worse for years. In less than six months, applying the principles described in this book, he had learned to understand and control the risk that created his pain. He realized in addition to pain control so much more had changed in his life. He didn't respond to everyday stimuli with his old depressed attitude. He was literally more up, not only in his body but in his attitude toward himself and others around him. Just yesterday one of Rogers co-workers (who, inspired by the changes in him, began studying with us) raved about what a difference it is to work with Roger now. Whereas his co-workers used to avoid him, now they all like him. He is also much more attractive. His head is poised on top of his spine, his spine is elongated and he moves with ease versus stiffness and strain.

Working on your own habits and patterns of movement is the way you can make a permanent change to protect yourself from strain. We have written this book in hopes that many people in a variety of occupations can recognize how they may begin to use the principles of Alexander Technique to enhance their life at work. Co-workers can support each other by sharing the tools this wonderful Technique offers to build a greater resilience in the face of risk, and to keep attitudes, levels of performance and wellness on the upswing. Supervisors can support health and safety in their work force, as well as in themselves.

We wish you all the ease, efficiency and fulfillment you have inherent within you. May this book and the Alexander Technique help you to discover all you are capable of being.

CHAPTER 1

Your Risk and Your Advantage

Stress levels are high in today's fast-paced work environments. Pressures and tensions get translated into tightening in our bodies and in our minds. "My neck and shoulders are so stiff by the end of the day." "I get headaches everyday at work." "My wrists hurt when I use a keyboard." "My job is overwhelming; I feel completely stressed out." If any of these phrases describe your experience, you are one of a rapidly growing number of workers in danger of developing injuries and diseases based on long term, cumulative stress.

Specialists say that one half of all Americans, that's 65 million people, are at risk for developing physical symptoms of work-related stress. These are called Repetitive Strain Injuries (RSI's). Repetitive Strain Injuries, such as carpal tunnel syndrome, tendinitis, sciatica, herniated or slipped disks, have risen to the top of the list as the most prominent occupational diseases. For you they can mean pain, medical expenses, loss of work time and income, limited life-style, and threats to your job security. For employers they can mean decreased productivity, absenteeism, escalating health insurance and disability costs, and sometimes law suits.

In response to these concerns companies have spent millions on specially designed office furniture, unions have lobbied for remedies, and business coalitions have been formed to address the problem. Yet despite diligent planning and investment, Repetitive

Strain Injuries continue to develop. Why? Because the only real prevention and cure begins with you and how you use your body in the workplace. Applying the principles of the Alexander Technique, you can learn how to prevent painful injuries and, in many cases, to recover without surgery. In *Working Without Pain* you will learn:

- What causes Repetitive Strain Injuries
- How to prevent the risk in your particular occupation
- How to discover the *Advantage* that will allow you to work and live with ease, efficiency and fulfillment.

What Is Your Risk?

In every occupation, stressful events and conditions are bound to occur. The fast pace of change in business and technology today has intensified levels of stress for many workers. What conditions in your job put you at risk of developing Repetitive Strain Injuries?

On the job, do you:
- Use a computer keyboard?
- Write frequently by hand?
- Use the telephone?
- Have quality and quantity quotas?

Office and communication workers are the group most at risk for common Repetitive Strain Injuries, such as carpal tunnel syndrome and sciatica.

Does your job require you to:
- Teach in classrooms full of energetic children?
- Follow a rigorous schedule?
- Work in understaffed conditions?

School teachers are subject to sustained physical, mental and emotional stresses that can spawn chronic injuries.

Does your work include:
- Responding to emergencies and crises?
- Lifting or moving people?

- Bending and reaching in odd positions to perform your work?

Doctors, nurses, and other medical professionals work in stressful conditions and often need to bear weight or assume awkward positions that can lead to chronic injuries.

Do you spend part or most of each day:
- Driving a car, truck, bus or other vehicle?
- Riding on a bus or subway?
- Frequently getting in and out of a vehicle?

For **commuters, cab drivers, truck and bus drivers, police officers, and sales representatives**, the seated position, the length of time behind the wheel, and getting in and out of a vehicle can pose substantial risk.

Does your job require you to:
- Stand long hours with arms reaching out to work?
- Reach your arms frequently above your head?
- Lift and carry baggage, parcels and packages?

The constant physical demands of lifting and carrying in the jobs of **package handlers** and **overhead workers** can spawn serious pain and injury. **Hairdressers, hygienists, assembly line workers**, who work with their arms continuously suspended and reaching out, can suffer from neck and shoulder injuries.

In each of these situations, there is a way to work without the risk of injury. Stress on the job or placing your body in taxing circumstances need not lead to pain and discomfort. In fact, you can use the challenges of your job to your advantage. The very circumstances that now place you at risk can be the opportunity for you to develop the *Advantage* that will change your life.

The Impact of Stress on the Body

Denise is a classic example of a worker at risk. As a Registered Nurse in the intensive care unit of a busy hospital, she finds herself constantly in the midst of crisis. She tends to victims of drunk-driving accidents and others with serious injuries who are brought into the emergency room clinging to life by a thread. The responsibility of her job literally weighed heavily on Denise's shoulders.

In fact, she found her shoulders felt stiff and ached most of the time. Certain that she had to accept such conditions in order to perform her job, Denise often went to work with acute pain in her back and neck. Because she feared the possibility of being black-listed by her supervisor, she said nothing and tried to ignore these warning signs of trouble. Denise was wearing down, but she couldn't see a way out. By the time she was referred to us by her doctor for the Alexander Technique, Denise had developed chronic low back pain, and she had a constant look of concern on her face. She carried her shoulders up around her neck, and she was unable to turn her head without pain. In fact, she moved as if her head, neck and shoulders were fused together.

Denise had been responding to the pain by holding her muscles even tighter, as if this might protect her. When we observed her usual way of standing, we could see that her pelvis and lower back were pushed forward, in response to the tightening in her shoulders and neck. Unfortunately, this attempt to relieve the pain and stiffness only perpetuated it and led to a tightness in her legs that, with each step, sent an impact to her back and spine. In reaction to stress and pain, our bodies typically respond, as did Denise's, in the following way:

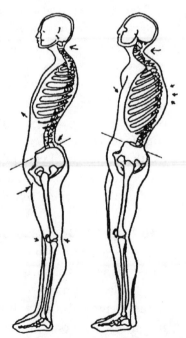

1. The head and neck tense to prepare for action.
2. In response, the spine stiffens.
3. Muscle tightening spreads throughout the entire body.

The force of this tightening strains and deforms the natural structure of the body. When we habitually respond in this way, our bodies begin to look like this:

The Consequences of Tightening and Misbalance

Figure A   *Figure B*

The Body at Risk

In both of these figures, tension in the neck causes the vertebra of the spine to compress. This distorts the naturally supportive curves of the spine which in turn weakens support for the whole body. In an attempt to compensate for the missing support, muscles in the rest of the body tighten.

The body's attempts to establish balance in response to distorted neck tension, is what we call "misbalance." In Figure A tension in the neck muscles have tipped the skull back and down into the spine. In response, a misbalance is created as the spine rounds and pelvis thrusts forward. This is the stance Denise had taken in response to stress.

Figure B illustrates a different and equally common response to stress. We frequently see this misbalance in those who use computers, as they thrust their heads forward toward the monitor and keyboard. When the head pulls forward and down, as illustrated, the cervical curve in the neck easily becomes over-straightened, placing a dangerous strain on the nerves and discs throughout the spine. The upper back rounds out and the pelvis moves back in misbalance.

Look at yourself in a mirror or ask a friend to observe you in your usual way of standing. Is it like either of the models in the illustrations above? Does your neck pull Back and Down as in Figure A, or Forward and Down as in Figure B? The Alexander Technique refers to this risky pattern of tension as "pulling down." In either of these two positions, your movement is restricted and your body is compensating through misbalance.

Compression of the spine, caused by contracting muscles in your neck and shoulders, exerts harmful pressures on the nerves that branch out from the spinal column, resulting in tension in other parts of the body as well. Repetitive strain problems will often begin when this response pattern occurs so commonly that it starts to feel normal. While you may grow accustomed to the feeling of misbalance, constant tension will maintain pressure and irritation on tissues around your joints and nerves which in time can lead to more severe symptoms.

Most RSI's originate with stress. Some experts say that a certain amount of stress may be good, and that certain people thrive under stress. However, for most workers stress is uncomfortable and potentially dangerous. What exactly is stress? Webster's Dictionary defines stress as: "a force exerted upon a body that tends to strain or deform its shape." What constitutes the force that is exerted upon your body in the workplace? While you might say that job quotas, deadlines, and continuous challenges are the cause of stress, these are actually just part of the multitude of stimuli we are responding to everyday.

Not everybody reacts in the same way to the same stimuli. For some people deadlines and challenges are incentives; for others they are distressful pressures. In fact, the force that "tends to strain or deform" the shape of your body is the result of how you react to such stimuli. While you may not have control over some of the circumstances in your environment, you can develop a way of responding that makes your life, at work and at play, more easeful and fulfilling.

What Is Your Advantage?

As Denise worked with the Alexander Technique, she quickly learned to recognize the cause of her injury and to change the ways in which she had been responding to the demands of her job. In simple basic movements such as sitting, standing and bending, she began to move her head, neck and spine in a new way. As she learned what it felt like to let her neck be free and to let her head come into balance on her spine, she became aware of how strained and awkward she was before she learned the Alexander Technique. She realized she had been unaware of her unconscious responses which had led to the stiffness throughout her neck and back.

As Denise became proficient in her new way of moving and responding, several things happened:

- Her neck became longer and she easily turned her head without pain.
- Her shoulders widened and moved with a noticeable looseness.
- Her back looked and felt longer and strain-free.
- Her spine and pelvis remained in balance with her head.
- Her leg joints bent easily when she walked.
- She felt an overall sensation of lightness in her movement.

Within a few weeks Denise was working without pain. Much to her surprise, even on the most hectic shifts at work, her level of stress was dramatically reduced. When you go about your daily routine with constant tension in your neck and back, it disrupts the natural potential of your body to function with poise and ease and puts you at risk of developing RSI's. Whether you work in a stressful environment like Denise, spend your day sitting at a desk, or find yourself frequently behind the wheel of a car. Your *Advantage* lies in simply discovering the natural coordinated and balanced relationship between your head, neck and spine. In the Alexander Technique, this is called your Primary Control.

The Primary Control

Due to his own voice problems in performance, F.M. Alexander took the initiative to study himself and experiment with what he observed. Using mirrors to help, he noticed that when he recited, his neck tightened, causing his head to tip back. This led to depressing his larynx, and gasping to breath. Along with this compressed shortening of his overall stature, he observed his chest lifting. He recognized this pattern of tension as being what was plaguing his voice.

Balance and Ease
The body with Advantage

Experimenting with different balances, Alexander discovered that his spine lengthened best and his voice was clearest when he achieved a "forward and up" balance of his head. This led to an important principle. He discovered that the dynamic relationship of the head, neck and torso is the primary element that affects human functioning. He called it the Primary Control. Alexander had discovered that in order to truly change troublesome patterns in his voice, he first had to balance his Primary Control.

When the neck is free and the head is balancing forward and up, the Primary Control is the most beneficial coordination in the human body. When the neck tightens and the head pulls back, the Primary Control is the most interfering coordination. The prevailing dynamics of the Primary Control immediately spreads to the rest of the body.

As you learn to bring your body into this beneficial coordination, you will begin to experience firsthand the balance and ease with which the body naturally moves. This is your Advantage.

The natural and healthy coordination of your Primary Control is:

1. Your neck, free from tension, allows your head to move forward and up in balance.

2. This in turn allows your spine to lengthen and back to widen.

3. Your body then acts efficiently without strain.

Your Advantage is in place when the muscles in your neck are at ease and your head, moving forward and up, leads your body in all actions. When your head leads with this balance, your body will follow with the least amount of strain. When you become proficient with this coordination, not only will your body work in a strain-free and pain-free balance, but other faculties, such as perception, comprehension and communication, will also improve.

What is the Alexander Technique?

Starting with the sense that he must be doing something to himself that was causing the loss of his voice in performance, F.M. Alexander discovered the importance of the Primary Control. A certain dynamic relationship of the head, neck and back can, if brought into operation integrate all bodily movement which improves functioning of the whole self as well as each specific part. As he continued to search for a solution to his own problem, he discovered a process that works to change the harmful automatic dynamics of the Primary Control to advantageous, balanced dynamics.

In stories and procedures throughout this book, we offer some of the techniques and methods we have successfully used over the last twenty years as teachers of the Alexander Technique. F.M. Alexander's method rests primarily on discovering the body's own natural coordination and the internal forces that affect it. Learning to apply the basic principles we offer with *Working Without Pain* can set you on the road to prevention of and recovery from injuries due to work-related stress.

Ergonomics Is Not Enough

In response to the problems generated by the modern workplace, an entire field of endeavor has developed. Ergonomics is "the science that seeks to adapt work or working conditions to suit the worker." This term is largely applied to furniture, workstation design, scheduling influences and task designs. Focusing on alleviating stress to the body, many companies have invested in costly desks, chairs and other equipment designed to prevent strain and injury. Yet, the incidence of RSI's has continued to grow.

The shortcomings of ergonomic furniture and equipment became clear to us during a tour we recently took of an insurance claims processing plant. Determined to create the best conditions possible for workers, the company had invested in expensive desks, chairs, keyboards, monitors and lighting for the data processors.

As we passed through one office, we observed a young woman in her 20's, sitting in one of these expensive ergonomic chairs. Despite the advantage the chair created for her, she was bending in the middle of her back, tightening her neck, and thrusting her head forward toward the computer screen. She looked like she was working hard to meet her quotas. This of course created a great deal of unnecessary tension throughout her body.

Risky misbalance and tension in a well-designed chair

Notice how you sit at your desk, or how you sit in your car seat while driving.

- Do you slide down in your chair?
- Is your neck craning forward from the rest of your spine?
- Can you detect accurately if your spine is in a vertical balance?
- Can you locate the joint where your head meets the top of your spine?

If you answered yes to any or all of these questions, you are already beginning to solve the problem by discovering what is causing risk and pain. Sliding down in the chair greatly distorts the supportive lengthening of the spine. When your neck is straining forward, it immediately triggers tension in the shoulders and back, further disturbing the dynamic balance of the Primary Control placing the whole body at risk. Most people we see believe they know when their spine is in a vertical balance with their head, and most discover their perception has mislead them. They have ended up creating an uncontrolled tightening in their backs to compensate for being out of balance. This misbalance has come to feel correct to them.

The location of the head on top of the spine is critical. However few people we have worked with know exactly where this joint is located. Most point to the back of their neck near the base of the skull. This response often correlates with the area from where their tension and pain originates. In chapter 5 you will learn to locate this critical joint and use it to your Advantage.

If you answered no to the above questions but still experience regular tension or pain, take the time to observe yourself more closely. What you think you are doing might be different from what you are actually doing.

Ergonomics can certainly help to reduce the effects of poorly designed work environments. However, regardless of how advantageously the work station is designed, it does not decrease the risk of RSI's if those who work there continue to interfere with their Primary Control coordination. As in all circumstances, the optimal use of ergonomically designed furnishings depends upon developing your Advantage by learning balance in your Primary Control.

Sitting with Balance and Ease - Advantage

In *Working Without Pain*, you will learn more about why and how the Primary Control gets out of balance. Through illustrated procedures, you will gain some tools that help learning how to establish and maintain your Primary Control in all the circumstances of your life. The tools and principles presented here will help you discover what you once knew—poise in action.

As children, we all had the potential for poise in our bodies and clarity in our minds. There are many reasons we lose this potential. The information and tools in this book will lead you to recover your birthright and prevent injuries and imbalance. Awareness of how you can use your body to your best advantage will result in new levels of self-control, enable you to stop pain and stress, and replace unwanted patterns that might be limiting your potential.

The first part of this book focuses on what Repetitive Strain Injuries are and what causes them. Next, we will explore the tools that lead to healing and prevention. Then you can choose the chapters that focus on the particular requirements of your job, although the principles and procedures in all the chapters have invaluable information for everyone. The conclusion of the book will lead you beyond healing and preventing injury into unfolding the fullness of your potential.

Thousands of people in all walks of life have learned the Alexander Technique, and overcome Repetitive Strain Injuries. From famous performers and athletes to ordinary people, the technique works with the strong appeal of common sense. If you could discover what you are doing that is causing stress and injury, would you want to stop it and thus stop the injury? Of course! And that is what you will begin to do through *Working Without Pain*.

CHAPTER 2

The Hidden Causes of Repetitive Strain Injuries

As we have seen in the last chapter, the particular physical actions required by a job certainly can lead to Repetitive Strain Injuries if performed inappropriately and under pressure. Aspects of the physical environment such as improperly-designed equipment and furnishings can also add to strain. Yet why does one individual suffer from the problem of RSI's while another, who works at the same kind of job, does not?

In 1992 a study was undertaken by the National Institute for Occupational Safety and Health (NIOSH) researching causes of RSI's among data entry workers at U.S. West Communications, a large telecommunications company. The study was sponsored by U.S. West Communications and the Communication Workers of America, a labor union.

The study included an extensive survey questioning workers about various aspects of their jobs. All those included in the research used efficient ergonomic chairs and desks, and the researchers took into account:

- Which city they worked in.
- Psychosocial factors.
- Electronic performance monitoring.
- Number of keystrokes per day.

In the end the researchers were unable to determine whether the number of key strokes per day either increased or decreased the likelyhood of Repetitive Strain Injury developing among those studied. However, they did determine that the conditions most strongly associated with the incidence of RSI's were what are called "psychosocial factors." These included but were not limited to:

- Fear of being replaced by a computer.
- Job insecurity.
- Work pressure.
- Work involving a variety of tasks.
- Lack of decision making.
- Lack of support from co-workers.
- Lack of productivity standards.
- Surges in workloads.
- Computer monitoring for quality and quantity .

This study clearly shows that, in addition to the physical circumstances that lead to RSI's, there are also what we might call "hidden" causes. Hidden causes may have little to do with the type of work you do or the physical environment in which you work. Nonetheless they have a major impact and contribute substantially to the risk of developing RSI's. These hidden causes can include the social dynamics of your working environment or psychological pressures you might be encountering in your personal life. You may bring with you from your past, consciously or unconsciously, ways of using your body which are stressful. You may be suffering from an injury that adds stress to how you function.

Workers are not "units of production" but human beings with a wide range of assets and needs, and they bring to work with them the history and circumstances of their lives. In this chapter, we will look at some of the hidden causes of Repetitive Strain Injuries— psychosocial stress, faulty messages from the past, impact of mental and emotional patterns, and habits developed due to structural differences or the residual effects of past injuries. One of the first and most basic steps you need to take in order to decrease your Risk and develop your Advantage is to recognize the full spectrum of factors that can lead to RSI's, including these important but too easily overlooked hidden factors.

Psychosocial Stress

Sandra is a bookkeeper for a school district. Her job includes extensive work with a calculator and making entries by hand in a journal. When she was referred to us to try the Alexander Technique for chronic tension and pain, she told us that operating the calculator was causing pain in her wrist, elbow and shoulder. We suggested she begin her process of recovery by observing how she held her body while she worked. A week later she was back to tell us that she habitually hunched forward at her desk to do her job, especially when she was reaching to use the calculator. Holding her body in this position involved a great deal of tightening. This tension, combined with the same tiny movements of writing and using the calculator spelled trouble.

Some experts profess that frequent repetition of the same small movements, as in using a calculator or writing, is what causes the strain that results in injury. Thus, RSI's are sometimes referred to as Repetitive Motion (or Movement) Injuries. The more repetitions that occur, these experts hold, the more likely injury will result. This is usually diagnosed as overuse. However, as we saw in the NIOSH study of data entry workers, clearly it wasn't the volume of keystrokes that was the determining factor in injury but rather the psychosocial stress. The context in which we work contributes as much to stress as the kind of work we do.

Sandra often faces critical deadlines as part of her normal workload. In addition, because her supervisor depends heavily upon her, she frequently is required to respond to last minute demands and take on unexpected rush jobs. That usually meant that the sustained repetitive movements she performed on her calculator and while writing were done with a great deal of tension and anxiety. The closer she got to a deadline, the more anxious and worried she felt, and the more tense her body became.

Understanding how the social pressure and psychological anxiety Sandra experiences translate into physical symptoms is the key to understanding prevention and cure. The principles of the Alexander

Technique describe the connection between stress in the environment and physical injury as a "psychophysical" phenomenon, having to do with the relationship between the mind and the body. Mental/emotional and physical states are interrelated. You have undoubtedly noticed this in your own responses.

- Do your shoulders and neck tighten when your work load feels overwhelming or when you are upset about something?
- Do certain people elicit a stressful reaction from you more easily than others?
- Do you end up feeling tense when you have to deal with unexpected changes?

Observe what happens to the muscles in your neck each time you encounter something unknown in your environment. This could be unexpected work demands, new learning situations, or even positive excitement. Do your neck muscles tighten, or do they relax? Reaction in your neck spreads to the rest of your body.

When some people are subjected to social or psychological challenges, they react by contracting. Tension in the head, neck and spine affects not only the entire body but also impairs judgment, perception and communication skills. This creates a vicious circle, as the attempt to compensate for imbalance creates even more imbalance.

The demands and pressures of Sandra's job were not going to go away. In lieu of quitting, she realized she could learn how to respond to the demands in a different, more balanced way. Since we cannot control everything in our environment, we basically have two choices in response to the inevitable changes and challenges we face: we can either work with them or resist them.

For many of us, tightening has become a habitual response over time. Fortunately, humans have the distinct ability to learn how to stop automatic reactions and substitute new ones. As she developed the tools of the Alexander Technique, Sandra began to recognize, moment by moment, when she was reacting stressfully and how. She noticed that when she tried to work harder, her neck tightened and shortened, causing her shoulders and head to draw towards each other. As she consciously released tension in her neck, it could lengthen, and her head and shoulders could move away from each other. She reported that this release would be followed by a light, easy quality in the movement of her arms. Not only did Sandra learn how to work with greater ease, she found she could work just as fast or even faster without becoming exhausted.

When stressful psychosocial factors in your work environment cannot be averted or avoided, you still have the choice to avoid harming yourself through them. As you learn how to change your responses to these factors, you decrease your stress and risk while also increasing your mental acuity.

Faulty Messages

Much of human behavior is learned through imitation. Consciously or unconsciously, we follow whatever models are provided. If the model is faulty, then the message we receive is likely to be faulty as well. If we learned ways of moving and responding with mis-balance and tension, our brains continue to send these messages to our bodies. So what becomes "normal" for us is not necessarily natural. By becoming conscious of faulty messages we have acquired, we can begin the process of correcting negative patterns and eliminating unnecessary causes of pain.

Unconscious Learning

One of our clients, Benjamin, had suffered from polio during childhood and was left with an obvious limp. Hoping to overcome his awkward and painful gait, he began learning the Alexander Technique. One session not long after he started, Benjamin brought his twelve-year-old son along with him. As they entered the room, we immediately were struck by the fact that the son had the same unmistakable limp as his father. However, he had never had polio or any other injury or disease that would have affected his legs.

Human beings are like sponges, continuously absorbing information and mannerisms from those around them. Without even being aware of it, individuals copy habitual responses and movement patterns of family members and peers. Even though a habit might be one of mis-balance or tension, we might adopt it and adapt to it so that it becomes normal to us.

Reflect on your own posture and mannerisms for a moment:

- Do you move or act like other members of your family?
- Have you ever unknowingly adopted someone else's mannerisms?
- At work, do you feel as tense as those around you might appear?

In the workplace, it is easy to pick up habits of tension in response to pressure to get work done. Without knowing it, you might find yourself becoming tense as you work on a project because your boss is tense and stressed out about the project. Recently, we walked into a big printing and copy business where there were six employees scurrying around hurrying to get work done. They all were tightening their necks and rounding their shoulders with stressed frowns on their faces. As we stepped up to the counter to be waited on, the manager helped us. She was very professional and knowledgeable but also maintained the same bodily attitude. Perhaps this was her way of using her body, and her employees had adopted it. Or perhaps she was adopting their bodily attitude.

Benjamin's son was not aware of the fact that he walked with a limp and was very surprised when we saw the video tape we made of him as he crossed the room. As they began to recognize that the limp had passed from father to son, they also realized that Benjamin was no more to blame for passing on this habit than his son was for picking it up. The entire process had been unconscious.

Fortunately, the boy once again followed in his father's footsteps by learning the Alexander Technique. Over the course of the next several months, they both discovered a way to move efficiently and comfortably. The son returned to his original capacity for grace and balance in walking, and the father learned how to move with ease, discovering that the limp he had walked with since childhood polio was not only harmful but actually unnecessary.

As you explore patterns of using your body that you may have unconsciously adopted from others, you will uncover faulty messages that may be putting you at risk for developing RSI's. We may also be influenced negatively by patterns we once consciously chose to develop or were actually taught to us.

Conscious Imitation

Ray came to us to learn the Alexander Technique because his chronic lower back pain had been returning often and persistently. We started working with him by asking him to take his "normal" stance and then walk back and forth across the room. As we watched Ray walk—pelvis forward, feet turned out, back swayed—we could easily see the source of his lower back pain. We asked him to focus on the way he felt as he stood and walked in his customary manner. Suddenly Ray recalled how, as a young teenager, he had idolized an older boy he thought was very "cool" and had consciously set out to imitate him. He taught himself to walk exactly like his idol. A little sheepishly, Ray acknowledged that this mimicking had undoubtedly been the cause of his back pain.

Stop for a moment to ask yourself:
- Did you teach yourself to move a certain way?
- Have you ever intentionally copied someone else's mannerisms?
- Have you considered that the way you learned to do a particular task may have been a faulty message?

Strainful misuse can actually be passed on during job training. In order to demonstrate aptitude, the learner will often perform a task exactly as he or she is shown. If a faulty message is being passed on, a worker's desire to do a good job may one day result in injury.

Laura worked as a sign language interpreter for three years before reaching the breaking point with pain and stiffness in her neck and shoulders. After months of physical therapy and consulting doctors, her pain was worse. She was desperately afraid of losing her career. A colleague of hers suggested she see us.

Laura arrived at our first meeting very skeptical that anything new might help, particularly something so simple as working with posture and movement. By the time she left the first session, she was able to move her head and neck with an ease and comfort she hadn't known in almost a year, and over the next few weeks, she made some significant discoveries about how and why her injuries began.

In one early session, we worked on how she used her body to sign with expression. As Laura demonstrated to us her customary movements, she realized that she was tightening her shoulders as she pulled her neck and head forward to emphasize a point she was making. At that moment of recognition, she stopped with a shocked look on her face and said, "That is how I learned to make such expressions. I copied my teachers and others." She also realized that she was reacting with excessive tension as she held her arms up while signing. Laura had consciously learned to use her body in this harmful manner, and the repetition of this pattern over the years had eventually resulted in her injury.

Mental and Emotional Patterns

Sylvia came to us with persistent pain in her neck and shoulders, hoping for some relief and also for help in improving her posture. Her shoulders were rounded, and she walked with a stoop. In our first session, when we guided her to discover her Primary Control, the release of tension in her neck and shoulders released her stoop. As Sylvia stood at her full height, she felt a dramatic sense of lightness. At the same time, however, she told us that she was feeling a great deal of resistance to this new experience because she had always felt self conscious about being tall.

Sylvia went on to recount how as a child she was unusually tall for her age, and taller than most of the boys in school while she was growing up. She had started shrinking down into her stoop, hoping to look shorter, thinking that maybe her height would be less noticeable. Surprising as it may sound, until that moment when she stood at her full height, Sylvia hadn't recognized that the imbalance in her posture had been a reaction to the emotional stress she felt about being tall. Connecting her mind and body together with a healthy Primary Control had unveiled the emotional link to her structural pain.

Individuals with serious emotional trauma in their history have come to learn the Alexander Technique, knowing it holds a particular key to their healing. While most have already worked extensively with counselors and psychotherapists, they have realized that aspects of trauma were still locked into physical patterns of tension in their bodies.

Mental and emotional patterns can develop from experiences and traumas throughout a person's life. When you bring these with you into work, your habitual responses may be compounded by the psychosocial stress of your current work circumstances. The same basic tools used to develop your Advantage, can also bring release to mental and emotional patterns.

Structural Differences and Injuries

Some of you may think, "Okay, I can change my attitude maybe, but I can't change how my body is made." Some individuals do have serious structural problems that can lead them to expect they will always have to put up with pain or stressful and awkward movements.

Jane came to study the Alexander Technique at the age of about 30, because of chronic headaches and pain in her shoulders and neck. She entered the room, walking with a pronounced limp that clearly generated a great deal of tension throughout her entire body. As we talked, she explained that at the age of twelve she'd had an accident in which she lost half of one foot. Doctors had told her that she could expect to have an aggravated limp for the rest of her life.

During her first session learning the Alexander Technique, Jane had an amazing discovery. After learning the Primary Control, she applied the new coordination to walking. When she stepped on the foot that had been injured, instead of moving her head forward and down, as she had done for years, she managed to send it forward and up. Her body followed by gliding forward smoothly. After some practice, Jane found that she had been limping needlessly, and that her chronic neck and shoulder problem had been related to the tension in her movement. Not only was she able to overcome the problem she had come in for, Jane learned that she no longer had to live by the limitations she had believed were permanent.

Injuries can result in persistent habits that may end up causing more pain than the original injury. Abbey came to the Alexander Technique with chronic intense pain in her shoulders and back which had started after suffering whiplash in an automobile accident several years before. A year after the injury, she began having painful spasms in her lower back. As she worked with the Alexander Technique, Abbey recognized that she was pulling her shoulders back and together in an attempt to protect them from the pain in her neck. This position created a misbalance that led to compression in her lower back, eventually resulting in spasms.

The pain from injury can provoke muscular holding around the pain. This is referred to as "guarding." The injury hurts, so you tense the surrounding area in an attempt to protect yourself from the pain. The tension aggravates the injury, leading to more pain, which stimulates more holding. And the cycle of pain goes on and on as the tension and associated mis-balance begins to feel normal. Such tension exerted upon the traumatized tissues can delay recovery from the injury or even prevent full recovery. Even if the injury heals, a set of unhealthy habits may lead to longer lasting problems and the risk of RSI's.

- Do you have pain from a previous injury?
- If you have been in an automobile accident, have you noticed uninjured parts of your body feeling weak or painful?
- Have you ever been diagnosed with scoliosis or other permanent structural condition that may pose limitations?

We have seen many people over the years who were told they could expect limitations and pain as a way of life. Once these people discovered the hidden factors that contribute to pain and limitations, they learned to function to their greatest potential without pain. Invariable they are surprised at how simple and effective the principles and procedures are to help them discover their freedom.

Faulty patterns of movement may begin through one or more of these hidden causes we have just looked at. Repetition drives the pattern deep into the nervous system, and over time a way of moving and responding that feels "normal" can lead to injury. Faulty messages can be reprogrammed with relative ease. In Chapter 4, you will be introduced to the tools that can help you begin.

The next chapter will give you an overview of the most commonly diagnosed RSI's as a way to enhance your awareness. Perhaps you will recognize work situations similar to your own and gain insight into risks you may currently be unaware of. Building awareness at work and early detection of symptoms is your strongest protection plan.

CHAPTER 3

Early Detection

Roberta came to us to learn the Alexander Technique because she was frightened that she might lose her job at a large data processing company. A few months earlier, she and others in her department had started hearing about employees in other areas of the company who had been diagnosed with carpal tunnel syndrome and had undergone surgery to correct it. Some of them still had pain after the surgery and were unable to return to their jobs. Then one of the data processors in Roberta's own department had been diagnosed with carpal tunnel syndrome and stopped coming to work. Soon after, Roberta and others in her department began to experience pain and strain in their wrists and forearms after several hours of entering data. To Roberta, as she told us, it seemed almost as if the symptoms were contagious, and she was concerned that she would end up diagnosed with carpel tunnel as well.

The "Epidemic" Phenomenon

This phenomenon, in which the reported incidence of a problem increases as workers hear about each others' problems, has come to be known as an "epidemic" in the workplace. While this "contagion" is not medically based, it could indeed be considered an epidemic of sorts. One or two people report symptoms of Repetitive

Strain Injury, such as carpal tunnel syndrome, and before long, more are reporting them. This can spread from a work-site in one city to a work-site in another, as workers travel or communicate with each other by phone about the problem. What is actually happening is that individual workers, aware that they are not the only ones experiencing discomfort at work, no longer sit by and quietly suffer as their symptoms progress to more serious stages. In other words, it gives workers permission to acknowledge a genuine and potentially dangerous circumstance. Some employers may consider such "epidemics" as psychosomatic excuses for paid leave from work. However, if approached intelligently and seen for what they are, an "epidemic" can in fact work for the benefit of everyone. By raising awareness of a problem in the making, an epidemic of symptoms functions as an early warning device which can lessen the impact of potential RSI's on workers.

It turned out that Roberta was lucky. When she first came to learn the Alexander Technique, it was clear that she had indeed been experiencing some early symptoms of repetitive strain. As she discovered what stress really is and how it contributes to RSI's, she also recognized how the fear of developing an injury had increased her stress, putting her even more at risk. Roberta concluded that discovering her own stressful physiological response was her key to recovery and to preventing further pain.

One of the best tools for reducing the impact of Repetitive Strain Injuries is early detection. The sooner you can identify the strain and discomfort which lead to RSI symptoms, the sooner you will be able to do something about them. When problems are approached in the early stages, they are more easily and quickly remedied. Many of our clients are referred to us by doctors for diagnosed RSI's. All of these injuries have had a long history of development. With the right information, it is possible to recognize early symptoms before they become injuries, and take preventative measures.

Progressive Stages of RSI

As we have seen, there are several factors that affect the development of Repetitive Strain Injuries: They include:
- Type of work or activity
- Psychosocial stressors in the workplace
- Personality and lifestyle
- Physical and psychological history

Early detection of RSI's begins with your assessing whether any of these factors contribute to your work experience. In reading Chapters One and Two, you have had the opportunity to consider each of these areas in relation to your own life. In this chapter, we describe the Repetitive Strain Injuries most typically found in the workplace, and note which occupations pose the greatest risk for developing each. While this list is no substitute for the advice of a physician, it can open your awareness and give you the information you need to prevent potentially serious injuries by developing your Advantage in face of risk.

Repetitive Strain Injuries do not develop overnight. The clues generally appear in symptoms very early on. There are three basic stages in which pain and tension progress to develop into an injury. Being aware of each stage may help you nip an injury in the bud.

Stage I: Tension builds up throughout the workday. At this stage you feel tired and have aching and soreness in the vulnerable areas. These symptoms go away during sleep and build up again the next day at work. When the warning sent by these early symptoms goes unheeded, the injury advances.

Stage II: Fatigue and pain begin to occur earlier on in the workday. While symptoms may still subside during sleep, pain occurs more frequently and tissues become inflamed. At this point, the actual RSI begins to develop. As tightening and guarding to "protect" the area of pain begins, habits develop that place constant strain on the weakened area.

Stage III: Pain is present during all waking hours and also during sleep. As pain interferes with restful sleep, fatigue increases. At this stage, pain is an inescapable trauma that interferes with the rest of life.

The more advanced the stage, the more difficult it is to remedy. Learning the Alexander Technique successfully at Stage I can free you of the injury and prevent future problems. Waiting until Stage III to help yourself means a much longer period of time for change and recovery.

Most of the people who come to us to learn the Alexander Technique are desperate. They've had a problem for months, if not more than a year, before they find us. They have tried cortisone shots, physical therapy, chiropractic, massage, acupuncture; if they're lucky, they haven't had surgery. Many of them are burned out from many appointments, week after week, for their problem. The principles of the Alexander Technique may appear too simple to have a powerful impact on such serious and complicated injuries. Yet with few exceptions, the majority who learn to apply the Alexander Technique during early stages of a problem, start to lose their symptoms and return to working without pain within two to four weeks. Why? Because they have finally addressed the cause of their injury, which is their own habitual misuse of the body. People with advanced stages, unfortunately take longer to reverse the damage, but also must stop the cause.

As we have seen in the previous chapters, there are overt causes that can lead to RSI's as well as hidden causes. No matter what the cause, with the Alexander Technique it is possible to overcome and prevent injury.

Commonly Occuring RSI's

Use the information in this list not as reason to worry but rather as an opportunity to begin helping yourself by building awareness of Risk in your work situation. The basic procedures and principles that bring healing to the individuals featured in each section are presented in the remainder of this book.

Tension Neck Syndrome, Cervical Syndrome

Most at risk: Typists, Key-Punch Operators, Cashiers, Cyclists and Couriers, Packers and Small Parts Assemblers Painters, Decorators, Dentist and Dental Surgeons, Cashiers, Data Entry Operators, Estheticians

Symptoms of Tension Neck Syndrome:

- Pain and stiffness in the neck
- Pain may extend down one or both arms
- Occasionally numbness in the hands
- Muscle tissue at the base of the skull may be swollen on one or both sides

Symptoms of Cervical Syndrome:

- Very difficult to turn the head
- Painfully stiff neck
- May be associated with degenerating discs or weakened joints in the upper spine

Tension Neck and Cervical Syndromes often develop as a result of habitual tightening of the neck before engaging in an activity. For instance, if while typing, bike riding or assembly work, you tend to tense your neck as if bracing for action, you may be at Risk for Repetitive Strain Injury.

Cervical syndrome is most often found in those involved in work in which they habitually strain the neck to look up or look down. Continuous strain in using the head and neck can dangerously impact already stressed discs and joints.

Mark is a painting contractor in his 30's. A major part of his work consists of looking up at eaves, ceilings, upper walls, and other areas requiring him to hold his head and neck in strained positions as he paints. After spending years with chronic pain in his neck and shoulders, he was diagnosed by his doctor as having Tension Neck Syndrome and was referred to the Alexander Technique. When he first came for a session, his upper back was rounded with a hunched appearance. We could see that his neck was pushed forward while the back of his head and shoulders were tightening towards each other. When we asked him to sit comfortably in a chair, the tension in his head, neck and shoulders continued. When we gently felt the back of his neck, the muscles just below the base of his skull were quite swollen. We could see that his physical movements were restricted. As we talked, Mark revealed that he had been athletic most of his life, and he now felt very unhappy about his loss of physical grace.

We set up the videotape equipment and handed Mark a paint roller with a long handle so he could simulate painting the ceiling. Afterwards, as we watched the tape with him, Mark could see for himself that every time he looked up to paint the ceiling, he thrust his neck forward and pulled his head back and down towards his shoulders. Each time he dipped his roller in the bucket for more paint, he sent his neck forward with great strain to look down at what he was doing. Mark had no idea that he had been moving like this.

As we guided him to discover how he was moving that was causing the painful condition, mark realized that he had been using the wrong joints to perform these movements. Instead of having his head move freely on the joint at the top of the spine, he had actually been bending and stressing the vertebra lower in his neck. As he became aware of how automatic this tense response had become, Mark was able to learn to stop when he headed into the destructive response and use his Advantage instead. As he became more accustomed to moving with his balanced Primary Control, the built-up tension in his neck and shoulders released and his neck and back began to lengthen. After a few weeks, Mark told us that his balance and movement reminded him of when he was a teenager. Not only did his neck injury clear up so that he could do his job without pain, he was also able to return to his athletic pursuits again.

Even though Mark was already suffering from a diagnosed RSI, he still benefitted by relatively early detection. As we have seen earlier, what happens in the head, neck and spine invariably affects the rest of the body. The problems he was experiencing would likely have gotten worse over time and triggered injuries in other parts of his body, such as the shoulders and low back.

Thoracic Outlet Syndrome

Most at risk: Painters, Porters, Overhead Assembly Workers, Truck Drivers, Hairdressers, Mechanics, Stockroom and Shipping Workers, Letter Carriers, Cashiers, Musicians

Symptoms:

- Numbness in the arms
- Tingling or burning sensation in the back or on the outside of the upper arms while moving them

This condition results from nerves and arteries between the shoulder and the neck being pinched. Some people simply have less space in their bodies for the nerves and arteries to pass through without obstruction and thus they are more easily stressed. Those whose work requires sustained reaching out with their arms are most at risk.

Michael makes his living playing banjo, and he likes to put a lot of soulful expression into his performances. The problem was that the stance he took in doing that created a lot of tension in his neck, shoulders and arms. He had gotten to the point where after even a short time of playing, he would feel extreme pain and numbness in his arms and hands. He feared that his next season of performance was actually in jeopardy.

We asked Michael to bring his banjo to his first session of Alexander Technique. Before anything else, we asked him to play his instrument for us while we filmed him on videotape. As he played, we could see his shoulders tighten forward; his neck strained as he pulled his head down toward his instrument. His collar bones looked as if they were locked in place, and the front of his chest was rigid. At the same time, his left arm was suspended in an awkward position as he moved his hand up and down the neck of his banjo.

Michael hadn't played very long before he reported discomfort and numbness extending down both his arms. Specifically, he reported a tingling and sometimes burning sensation down the outside of his upper left arm as he moved it along the frets of his banjo. Suspecting that his problem could become quite serious, we recommended that he see a qualified doctor for an accurate diagnosis, while he continued working with the Alexander Technique to help him recover and to prevent further problems. The doctor reported that if Michael were to continue playing his banjo without correction of the strain, he could very well end up with full-blown thoracic outlet syndrome, which would not only be very difficult to overcome but would also put Michael out of work. Fortunately, Michael's symptoms were in an early stage, and were present only while playing his instrument.

As Michael observed himself on video and while playing in front of a mirror, he recognized what was causing his injuries. However, it was difficult for him to believe that he could experience and convey the same artistic expression without the usual rather dramatic posture that he had become accustomed to. However, considering the circumstances, Michael didn't have much choice, but to learn another way—one without tension in his neck, shoulders and arms.

As he learned the Advantage awareness and coordination, he began to apply it to playing the banjo. Although it felt awkward, and sometimes even "wrong" to him, Michael stuck with it, adjusting his performing style. When he had established his Advantage in performance, we filmed him again while playing his instrument. This time when Michael watched the video, he was surprised and very pleased to see how poised and expressive he looked in his new style. The biggest bonus was that his pain and numbness stopped and has not returned, and he has gone on to many more successful performance seasons.

Rotator Cuff Tendinitis and Bicipital Tendinitis

Most at risk: Construction workers, Welders, Painters, Hair stylists, Estheticians, Musicians, Window washers, Assembly workers, Stockroom and Shipping Clerks

Symptoms:
- Pain especially when moving the arm in an arc from just below the shoulder to just above the shoulder; sometimes in other movements as well

- Sometimes accompanied by pain, weakness and numbness extending down the arms and, in some cases, into the hands

Rotator cuff tendinitis is an inflammation in the tendons of the shoulder muscles. Bicipital tendinitis is also in the shoulder area and often occurs at the same time as rotator cuff tendinitis, with very similar symptoms. The tendons in these areas become inflamed and painful due to excessive tensing in action, especially when reaching. The problem occurs primarily in people who must hold their arms up and away from their body for extended periods of time, although other strained arm positions can also cause this Repetitive Strain Injury. Those who spend most of their working day with their arms extended, using tools or carrying and moving objects, are most at risk.

Christine has been a hairdresser for 24 years. She began experiencing pain and weakness that started in her right shoulder and extended down her arm and into her hand. At first she felt the symptoms only at the end of each day and she thought they would diminish on their own. By the time we met her, eight months after the symptoms began, the pain was constant, and she had to take pain pills to go to sleep. Every morning the pain was still present when she woke. Christine had consulted numerous medical professionals and had been diagnosed with Shoulder Tendinitis. While she had gotten temporary relief from prescribed drugs and from massage, her symptoms weren't going away. A doctor advised her that the only solution was surgery to remove part of the bone so the tendon would not have to stretch around it. There was no guarantee, however, that this would solve the problem. It was at this point that a friend of Christine's encouraged her to try the Alexander Technique.

When Christine first spoke with us, she pointed out that she was acutely aware of extreme tension throughout her whole body which she felt was somehow directly related to the pain in her shoulder and arm. We agreed with her that it was indeed related, and we set to work to introduce the Advantage that could bring her relief. As Christine demonstrated how she normally moved as she worked on the hair of a client, we observed that she was leaning backwards with an arch in her lower spine. This imbalance caused her to stretch and strain her shoulders in order to raise her hands. This meant that the inflamed tendon was in fact stretching and rubbing around the bones of her shoulder.

In her first lesson, Christine learned the Advantage coordination along with balanced bending in her knees. To her amazement, when her lower back was vertical to her head and she raised her arms, they felt lighter and hardly hurt at all. But to Christine it felt as if she was bending forward, even though she was upright. Although this position felt very confusing at first, the reduction in pain motivated her to continue applying this new coordination and balance. Within a few weeks, Christine was actually working without pain. She had avoided surgery and discovered a solution that released the tension she had carried throughout her body due to the imbalance in her Primary Control.

Epicondylitis

Most at risk: Computer Operators, Small Parts Assemblers, Musicians, Construction Workers, Woodworkers, Golfers, Tennis Players

Symptoms:
- Pain leading from the elbow to the wrist
- Neck and shoulder problems

Epicondylitis is one of the Repetitive Strain Injuries most common among computer operators. Some doctors consider it an early stage of Carpal Tunnel Syndrome. The condition is associated with repeated and forceful rotation of the forearm, or from using the arm with the elbow in a stiff fixed position. Pain in the forearm arises from the inflammation of the tendons between the elbow and wrist, actually originating with tension in the neck.

Nick is a school teacher and an avid kayaker and cross country skier. He had come to the point, however, where he hadn't been able to participate in any of these activities without pain and tension. Diagnosed with epicondylitis, Nick was referred to the Alexander Technique. He reported pain in his forearms but, not surprisingly, also tension and discomfort in his shoulders and neck.

When Nick came for his first session, his neck was so tight that when we asked him to turn and look to his right, he couldn't do so without turning his body as well. When we asked him to pick up a book from the table, we noticed that his neck became even tighter and his shoulder and whole arm stiffened with the action. Clearly, we needed to work with both his neck and his arms. His neck was stiff and shortened, causing it to curve forward excessively. When he became aware of this holding pattern, we guided him in some procedures to learn how to let his neck be free and allow his head to move at the hinge at the top of his spine. We also suggested that he let his elbows hang loose whenever he began bending his arms to reach for something. In contrast to his usual stiffening to begin reaching, he learned to release tension in order to move his arm. Nick took this information and spent the next week at work focusing on the movement of his neck and arms.

When he returned a week later, Nick commented that his level of stress in the classroom, which was usually high and continuous, had been much lower. He said he had enjoyed his students during that week in a way he hadn't for a long time. In addition, his elbow had been bothering him far less. During the course of that week, Nick had realized that whenever he felt stressed, it manifested in his shoulders and neck. The level of tension he had felt there had been so distracting that he hadn't been noticing he was tensing in his elbows and hands as well.

As he continued with the Alexander Technique, Nick learned other ways to reach and use his arms with Advantage. The surprising results were that even during his recovery period, he was able to engage in kayaking and cross-country skiing—activities that usually aggravated and inflamed his elbow. Eventually, he rid himself of the pain altogether.

Carpal Tunnel Syndrome

Most at risk: Key-Punch Operators, Typists, Assembly Workers, Musicians

Symptoms:

- Pain in the wrist and hand
- Tingling and prickling on the skin of the wrist and hand
- In more advanced stages, fine motor movements become difficult, muscle function is weak and impaired

Carpal tunnel syndrome is a condition that occurs when the median nerve is entrapped and compressed by surrounding tendons as it passes through the wrist. The problem is associated with hand movements and positions that are forced and repeated.

This is such a common RSI that if you have not experienced it yourself, you probably know friends or colleagues who suffer from a stage of it. Carpal tunnel syndrome is a painfully disabling injury when it gets to advanced stages. Often surgery is recommended to release the stress on the entrapped nerve. One of our acquaintances pursued this avenue for recovery only later to find the pain returning. Shocked and dismayed, she said to us, "My doctor said this would take care of it." She turned pale when we told her that we had talked to a number of people who'd had surgery as many as four times and still had the disease. The reality is that surgery does not stop the cause of carpal tunnel syndrome.

Lee works as a support technician for a software company and spends most of his work time at the computer. He also is a performing musician and likes to practice guitar and violin at least one to two hours per day. We have known Lee for a number of years and were surprised to see him with wrist braces when he came to us for help. He told us he had begun to feel pain everyday in his wrists and hands at work and that it was nearly impossible for him to play music anymore. His doctor had referred him to see us before the pain progressed any further. While the doctor had said the symptoms weren't severe enough for full diagnosis as carpal tunnel syndrome, he told Lee that if he didn't change the way he was doing things, the problem could easily advance to that stage.

During the first visit, we had Lee remove his wrist braces. We asked him to sit before a table and reach his hands up to the table top as if it were a keyboard. The first thing he did, even before moving his hands and arms one inch, was tighten his neck and shoulders. As he positioned his hands at the imaginary keyboard, we observed the neck and shoulder tension extend down his arms and into his fingers. When we asked Lee if he noticed this, he said no, that it just felt normal.

We immediately began to guide him to discover how free his neck and shoulders could be, and how to coordinate his arm movement with equal ease and freedom. As he followed our guidance, Lee could hardly believe how tight his neck had normally been and that he wasn't even aware of it. The contrast of his new Advantage coordination with his former tension helped Lee recognize the harm in his habit. He learned how to apply his Advantage to sitting in a chair, and he learned the Lying Down Procedure (see Chapter 4), which we suggested he do everyday for twenty minutes during the following week. We also suggested he continue to be aware of how he was using his body, and each time he noticed the tension to consciously put to use what he had learned about his new coordination.

Lee arrived at his second visit without his wrist braces. He told us he had taken them off because his wrists were not as painful. He was still tightening his neck, shoulders and arms, but not as much. Lee said he was now aware of how much tension he held in his shoulders at work. While the lessening of the pain was welcome news, we considered his awareness of his tension the major improvement for the first week.

During the second week, he continued every day doing the Lying Down Procedure and other procedures we introduced. The more he did these, the more he noticed about the way he used his body at work and while playing music. When Lee returned for his third visit, he said that his wrists didn't hurt at work any more, but his left hand still was in pain when he played the guitar. He brought his guitar with him, and we asked him to play it for us. He sat down and placed the instrument in his lap. As he started to play, his neck, shoulder and arm tension returned, straining his left hand as it moved up and down the guitar's neck. We asked Lee to stop playing and guided him to again apply his Advantage coordination to sitting in the chair. We asked him then to play again, this time putting attention on keeping his neck free and relaxed.

When Lee tried to position his guitar this time, he found it very awkward because his Advantage created a different shoulder and arm balance. We suggested that he try positioning his instrument to complement his Advantage. He found it quite strange to do so. Nonetheless, Lee applied this new instruction everyday during the next week. When he returned for his fourth visit, he brought his guitar to show us his playing again. He reported that by the end of the week, his left hand had started feeling significantly more free and easy. Lee had made enough improvement to get him out of pain and to increase his awareness of his habitual tightening response. Over time he continued learning more and has successfully avoided the devastation of carpal tunnel syndrome that he had come so close to developing.

Herniated and Deteriorated Discs

Most at Risk: Drivers, Desk Workers, Manual Laborers, Delivery People

Symptoms:
- Can cause pain in the immediate area of the disc
- Can cause pain, numbness or weakness extending down the arms and legs

Herniated or deteriorated discs can occur at any point along the spine. Disc damage can be the result of an accident, but more often it is caused by continuous, undue tightening and bending in the spine that force its natural curves to become exaggerated or over-straightened. With tension on the vertebra, the discs, which act as a cushion between each vertebrae, become either worn down or "herniated," squeezed out of the area between the vertebra. Consequently, nerves become pressed upon and irritated. In some cases, the vertebra rub directly against each other, causing calcification or bone spurs which also create irritation on the nerves.

These stresses on the spine result when the head, neck and spine tighten, leading to the tightening of other major joints. When the hip joints and the head-neck joints are restricted in movement, inappropriate bending takes place in the vertebra. This can happen with both simple movements and forceful movements.

Albert is a realtor who divides his worktime between driving around in his pickup truck looking at properties and sitting at a desk doing paper work. One day when driving on a street in town, he glanced back over his shoulder before merging left and suddenly experienced a shocking pain from his neck and upper back shooting down his arm. His doctor told him that he was suffering from a herniated disc in his upper spine, and that he should watch it closely over the next three weeks. During the next few days, Albert discovered that he had lost power in his hand grip, and he could no longer engage in his favorite pasttime, golf. Back again to see his doctor, Albert learned that the disc was deteriorating and if symptoms did not improve, he would need surgery. The fortunate part of all this was that Albert's doctor referred him to us for the Alexander Technique.

During Albert's first three lessons, he learned his Advantage coordination and especially how to apply it to driving his vehicle. By the third lesson he was getting relief from the pain in his arm, but his grip remained weak. In the fourth lesson he learned how to combine healthy arm movement with his Advantage coordination. By this time Albert's doctor had confirmed that his spine was improving and told him that at this rate of recovery, he could avoid surgery. Over the next weeks, Albert faithfully reviewed his Alexander Technique guidance and procedures on a regular basis.

By the eighth week after his "accident," the strength in his grip was returning, his pain was gone, and his doctor said he was no longer in danger of needing surgery. Albert has returned to playing golf again, and he continues with the Alexander Technique as a preventative.

Sciatica and Low Back Pain

Most at Risk: Those who drive for a living, Mechanics, Office Workers, Couch Potatoes, Body Workers

Symptoms of Sciatica:

- Pain and/or numbness in low back or hip, extending down the leg to the foot
- Pain and numbness may also occur in distinct rather than continuous areas

The sciatic nerve originates in the lower spine and passes through the pelvis and down the leg. Sciatica is the affliction of this nerve. In most cases, the nerve is irritated at the point where it branches out from the spine (often associated with disk problems or calcification) or where it passes next to or through the deep muscles of the pelvis. Irritation is often caused in these points by tense and mis-balanced movement which places constant pressure on the sciatic nerves.

Phil is a policeman and spends most of his worktime cruising in a patrol car, on the look-out for trouble and potential danger. By the time he was referred to us, he had pain in his low back which was also shooting down the side of one leg. When we asked him to sit in a chair, we could see that he tucked his pelvis under, thus creating a rounding in the lower part of his back. In addition, his neck was tightening forward and pulling down towards his legs, which rounded his shoulders. When we pointed out that this relationship of his neck and spine was harmful, Phil was very skeptical that the balance of his head and neck could have anything to do with his low back pain and sciatica. How could sitting a little differently have any effect!

We asked Phil if he would be willing to follow the slight suggestions from our hands as we guided his neck and head to release tension. As we did so, he let his head ease up to balance on top of his spine. Immediately, his spine and back became longer and he found himself sitting up taller in his chair—all of this completely without tension. Suddenly Phil remarked that his low back and leg pain were gone. As soon as we stopped guiding him, he returned to his previous position and the pain returned. Surprised, Phil said, "Teach me how to do that!" We spent the entire first lesson on Phil learning his Advantage coordination and applying it to sitting. As soon as he let his head move forward and up he could immediately feel the discomfort in his lower back lessen greatly. By the end of the lesson, he understood how the organization of his head, neck and spine could turn the pain on and off.

With this new information, Phil went back to work and started observing which circumstances he tensed under. He noticed his head pulling down toward the steering wheel as a response to tension. Each time he stopped that response, he avoided the pain in his back and leg. As Phil continued learning the Alexander Technique, he applied his Advantage to walking, bending in movement and also in his exercise program.

Hip, Knee, Ankle & Foot Problems

Most at Risk: Delivery People, Aerobic Instructors, Those who work on their feet, Those who bend and lift, Those who move up and down steps repeatedly

Hip, knee, ankle and foot problems are easily recognized by the symptoms of pain in those specific areas. The actual conditions that give rise to pain can include tendinitis, bone spurs, ligament damage and deterioration of bone and joint tissues. When people let problems in the leg joints go too long without correcting the cause, the results can be quite serious. In some industries, hip replacements, and surgeries for knees and feet occur for workers who are only in their early 40's. Again, correcting the initial cause—misbalance in the body—is the surest way to avoid debilitating conditions.

In some cases, misuse of the body is in no way apparent. We have found this particularly true in working with aerobic instructors who have come in with leg-related work injuries. These are women and men who have been trained professionally in certain postural exercises and work with particular attention to good posture in their aerobic dance as well as weight training. When Vicki came to us, referred by her doctor, her right knee was inflamed more or less all the time, and teaching seemed to make it worse. She was very concerned that she was going to have to cut back on her teaching schedule, which would represent a financial hardship. We asked her to put that decision off until she had completed one or two Alexander Technique lessons.

We started by observing Vicki's usual way of standing, sitting, walking and bending, and then asked her to show us some of the dance routine she found stressful. At first sight, Vicki's body looked straight and strong and appeared to be in good alignment. However, we began to notice a major flaw. As she moved, Vicki's neck was contracting in back, causing her chin to stick up and out. This was constant in all of her movement. When we explained to her that her head and neck coordination was the source of a harmful tension that extended down to her knees and feet, Vicki was very skeptical. We proceeded to guide her into her Advantage coordination while she was sitting and then standing. Without neck tension, her head balanced differently and all the movements and positions felt very queer to Vicki. When she viewed herself in the mirror in her new coordination, she said she didn't look anything like she felt. She looked very poised and upright but felt like she was bending forward. As she applied her Advantage to walking, Vicki commented that she felt very light and her knee hardly bothered her at all. Yet as soon as she went back to her ordinary pattern of walking the pain increased. We suggested she work this new information and coordination into her teaching routines. At the second visit, Vicki was pleased to report that she had not had to slow down her teaching schedule and was having far less pain. By her third lesson, she was pain free.

During her six visits to our office, Vicki concentrated on learning and applying the Alexander Technique procedures to her dance instruction. This had a lovely carry over into her other daily activities and movements. By her final lesson, Vicki had developed a keen awareness of when she was losing or gaining her Advantage coordination in almost all of her activities.

Beginning with Awareness

With Alexander Technique, recovery and prevention are one and the same. As you have seen in the above stories, getting out of pain may not take very long. It may take you a little longer to establish your Advantage as a preventative in order to ensure that risk and injury do not occur or reoccur. The brief amount of time it takes to learn the procedures can save not only hours but perhaps the weeks or months of time were you to become incapacitated through Repetitive Strain Injury. In any case, the time you put into learning the Alexander Technique pays off in the improved quality of your life.

Questions to Identify Your Risk

Recognizing early signs of tension or pain is important in identifying potential RSI's. In reading this chapter, you have discovered some symptoms to pay attention to in your own work. To identify your risk most accurately, consider the following questions while you are doing your job. Pause at different times of the day to notice what your answers would be.

- Do you experience pain, tenderness and stiffness in the neck muscles, both deep and superficial?
- When turning or moving your head, do you feel pain, or a restricted range of motion in your neck?
- Are spasms in the muscles between your head and upper back common?
- Are your shoulders chronically tensed forward with stiffness around the collar bones?
- Do you sometimes experience numbness down either arm?
- Does tension build in your shoulders and turn into pain on some days?
- Are you losing flexibility and range of motion in your arms?
- Do your elbows hurt after playing games like tennis, golf or bowling?
- What happens to muscle tension in your arms when stress at work increases?

- Do you bend in your lower spine when you should be bending at your hips?
- When you bend to pick up an object, do you tighten your legs and bend your back first?

As you consider these questions during your daily actions, you are already helping yourself, regardless of what your answers are. This is the first step in developing an accurate and trustworthy awareness of your actions. In the next chapter, we will look at how awareness and other basic tools for change are your first steps in preventing risk and injury.

CHAPTER 4

Tools For Change

Jennifer is a classic example of the worker at risk in today's business climate. Before beginning her career in publishing, Jennifer had been used to being physically active throughout the day. Her new career, on the other hand, kept her primarily in front of a computer. She always had deadlines to meet so she worked as fast as she could. Even though Jennifer considered herself healthy and physically fit, by the end of every working day, she felt tired. Her neck, shoulders and upper back felt stiff and tense. On some days, she developed a headache, something that had rarely occurred in the past. On extremely stressful days, Jennifer experienced symptoms of the asthma she thought she had left behind with childhood. Although she was only in her 20's, Jennifer was beginning to feel as if her health was breaking down.

With the advancement of technology comes the reduction in the need for physical movement, and an increase in expectation of speed and efficiency. These factors have placed a continually increasing demand on workers. For decades labor leaders have acknowledged this trend. In 1937 Ernest Begin in his Presidential Address at the British Trade Union Congress stated: "The nation has awakened to the fact that too great a price can be paid for the mad rush to increase production. Notwithstanding all the money which has been spent to cure known diseases, industry is constantly creating others." (Reported in *The Daily Herald*, London,

December 7, 1937). Repetitive Strain Injuries are among these new diseases. In this chapter we will look at the Tools for Change you need to protect yourself against them.

In our culture, we tend to believe that we have to be tense in order to achieve our highest level of performance. Picture the first grader writing her name. With all her might, she grips her pencil, squints her eyes, and hunches down close to the desk. Concentrating hard, she proceeds to write her name on the proper line. Her body is contracted and stiffened. Her mind is narrowly focused. We are taught early on that concentration and trying hard will pay off. What we are not taught is that a broadened Awareness and a more balanced muscular state achieves the best results. Realizing that her tense and furious pace was harmful, Jennifer came to us for the Alexander Technique to see if there was a different way to approach her work. She found that when she experienced the Advantage co-ordination in her first session, the tension in her neck, shoulders, arms and hands disappeared. But as soon as she returned to work, she went right back into her old patterns.

Many of our clients find that it is easy enough to learn a new and relaxed coordination in their body when they are in a session with us or practicing their procedures at home. But how do they apply this information when they are responding to the demands of work, when they are in the midst of the very pressure that brings up the tense response?

The Alexander Technique has three guiding principles of change that apply exactly to these circumstances. They are Awareness, Pause and Direction. In this chapter, we will look at how you can use these basic tools to correct habits that put you at risk and establish the Advantage that will prevent you from developing Repetitive Strain Injuries.

Awareness

When a major demand arises at work, do you tend to feel more tense as you attempt to meet it? Under pressure, most of us forget about ourselves—about how our bodies, our minds, our emotions feel—and focus only on the demands placed upon us by our circumstances.

"I can't think about myself at work, I'm too busy. There's too much else to think about." We hear this response quite often when we first introduce the concept of Awareness to people coming in for help with the Alexander Technique. People typically think they must forget about themselves to meet the demands of work. This is where the problems begin. Understanding how our Awareness functions is the first Tool for Change.

Each person has two basic fields of Awareness:

1. Perception of other people, physical surroundings, deadlines, events, and other external stimuli.
2. Perception of how they are responding to their environment: with tension and misbalance or balance and ease.

At every moment we are responding consciously or unconsciously to our environment; that is, we are aware of our responses, or we are "on automatic," unaware of how our bodies and minds are reacting. As we saw in Chapter 2, faulty messages can become part of our automatic response. This faulty response becomes a problem because the tension and misbalance feel normal or right. Sometimes it may even feel necessary. The Primary Control—the dynamic balance of the head, neck and spine—is at the core of this problem. All coordinated response begins here. If we start movement with the neck and head pulling down—tightening and shortening the head neck and spine relationship—the balance of the entire body is adversely affected. When this habit of pulling down feels normal, our Awareness is no longer sending and receiving accurately the information that we need for health and balance. This is called faulty sensory perception.

Everybody has at least six senses. In addition to touching, tasting, smelling, hearing and seeing, another essential sense which we all use is kinesthesia. This sense, associated with the muscles, tendons and joints, perceives physical position in space, movement, balance and tension in different parts of the body. Most of us have learned little or nothing about this sense, yet we began using it as infants and without it we could not walk without bumping into objects, we couldn't get a spoon to our mouth, and we couldn't detect whether our bodies are holding tension or not. By becoming aware of and developing your kinesthetic sense, you can identify when and how muscular tension and misbalance start as part of the way you do things. This is the key to learning how to stop tension and misbalance and to learn ease and balance.

Bill is a good example of someone who benefited from developing his kinesthetic Awareness. Bill is a dispatcher at a small taxi company. Talking on the phone while writing is one of his primary work activities. Bill first needed to become aware of the tension in his habitual way of performing these tasks before he could begin to perceive, with his kinesthetic Awareness, a healthier and more relaxed coordination.

When Bill started learning the Alexander Technique, we asked him to perform his usual task of answering the telephone and writing down information. As he used the phone, we observed Bill pull his head down and twist his neck. When he grabbed the pencil to write, he tightened his hands, arms, shoulders and neck. When we pointed out both of these actions to him—bringing them into Bill's Awareness—he realized that he had been so concerned with getting information written down that he had never stopped to realize what he was doing with his body. The thought flashed through Bill's mind that, up to this point, it had seemed necessary to tighten in order to write and that a sense of tension felt right in order to work better and faster. He had a profound realization that other simple, daily activities in his life were also plagued by the same guiding sense of tension feeling normal and right. Bill had discovered that faulty sensory perception lay behind his pain and discomfort at work. The very habits that felt right were the ones that were put- -

ting him at risk. One of F.M. Alexander's important principles is that in recognizing your faulty Awareness, you can begin to discover how it keeps you stuck in tension and misbalance. Then you can use conscious Awareness to correct it.

When Bill recognized these risky patterns of tension and realized how they caused pain in his hand and wrist, he was ready to make the changes needed to be at ease at work. To further develop his Awareness, Bill learned the Advantage of ease and balance. When he managed to let his neck be free from tension and his head balance forward and up, he found that writing felt distinctly strange and abnormal but strain-free throughout his neck, shoulders and arms. This initial, brief experience was encouraging to Bill, but it was hard for him to believe that he could use it at work to affect his performance.

There was a three-hour period each day at work that was the busiest and most tense for Bill. After this time he invariably felt tense and achy. Although he felt dubious, Bill decided he would take the chance and give priority to being aware of his body while he was working during that tense three-hour period. The first time he did it, he felt like he was moving far too slowly. Nevertheless, he persisted with self-Awareness, noticing his habitual risky behavior and over and over adjusting back to his healthy Primary Control. By the end of the busy period, everything had been accomplished on time and with no problems. Best of all, Bill felt calm and at ease.

One of the keys to establishing your Advantage is to use the Primary Control as a sensory feedback tool. Rather than trying to keep track of whether there is tension throughout your entire body, you can direct your attention to your head, neck and shoulders. As we have seen, what happens here affects the rest of the body. Once your Awareness is no longer misled by faulty messages and has been awakened to what a healthy Primary Control feels like, it can alert you to when you are pulling down in your head, neck and shoulders and guide you back to your Advantage.

Pause

The key to Bill's ability to reprogram his faulty Awareness lay in his ability to withhold his automatic response. This skill, which F.M. Alexander called "Inhibition," is the second basic and powerful Tool for Change that you can use to develop your Advantage. When you Pause, you can stop your habitual response to stimuli and in its place establish your healthy and beneficial Primary Control. A stimulus can be as apparently simple as sitting in a chair moving your fingers on the keyboard, or as complex as handling a crisis. It can be a stressful deadline or dealing with competition in the work place. How you respond to stimuli shapes the quality of your thoughts and actions. You can react or you can choose to respond in order to achieve more effective results.

Whenever you begin an action, your body responds by assuming a postural set. Notice whether you prepare for an activity by rigidly fixing your body and attention to the task ahead. For example, think about when you reach to answer the telephone. Do your neck, shoulder and arm tense as you begin reaching?

To Pause means to stop or inhibit habitual response. When you become aware that you are reacting by tensing and pulling down in your Primary Control, the next step is to Pause for a moment to interrupt the harmful habit. This ability to Pause and withhold response is a valuable skill that starts in your nervous system. The more you practice it, the better you get at it.

When Jennifer returned to work after her first Alexander session, she began to practice the Tools for Change. She started noticing that the harder she worked, the more she would pound on the keyboard, tensing her hands, with the accompanying strain up into her arms, shoulders, neck and head. Each time she became aware of this habitual response, she Paused. This helped to build her Awareness of the misbalance and tension.

During this Pause, she released the tension in her neck, allowing her head and shoulders to ease away from each other. The cumulative effect of repeating this many times during each day was that the pain in her neck and arms began to disappear. She felt much less tension in her neck, and her asthma attacks stopped.

The initial Pause simply interrupts habit. Using this Tool ten to twenty times a day will begin to make a difference in your work experience. In pausing, you are allowing your neck and head to be free of tension, and the rest of the body follows. Formerly difficult tasks can become easier as you stop adding to the difficulty by responding with tension.

Direction

The third Tool for Change that you need to help you gain your Advantage has to do with clearly establishing the Direction in which you want to go, which is a healthy Primary Control. When you let your neck and head be free of tension, ideal tone is triggered throughout the body. Ideal tone is present when the least amount of contraction is used to accomplish movement. When the head eases forward and up, the body follows by releasing tension. This release of contraction down the spine results in the spine reaching it's greatest length.

The spine lengthens by releasing muscles not contracting them. You may feel lighter when this happens because tension throughout the joints is lessened. Such tone allows greater speed and efficiency in body movement because there is less resistance. The head is free to balance and lead when the muscles stop contracting. Rather than trying to contract muscles to coordinate movement, you must learn to release muscles to coordinate movement. In all of your movements, your Advantage means: your head leads and the body follows.

Coordinating words and actions are an essential part of moving in your new Direction. To establish your Advantage coordination, as you do each action, say to yourself:
- Let my neck be free
- Let my head balance forward and up
- Allow my back to lengthen and widen
- Let my head and neck remain free

Visualize each of these actions as you say the words to yourself. Seeing an inner image of each action further empowers your ability to do it. Repeating the specific words in specific order is also essential. These words are the orders that you are training your body to follow. As you repeat the words along with the visualization, your body will follow with no effort.

We have had new students come back to us to report that their necks and backs feel stiffer and more painful since starting to learn the Alexander Technique. When we ask them how they are enacting what they have learned, we usually find out that they are not repeating the words to themselves, and most often they are trying to "feel their way" to holding their heads correctly. Therein lies the problem. As you have learned by now, your sensory Awareness can play tricks on you. Instead of trying to "feel your way" to holding your head "right," you must at first become aware of your risky coordination, Pause, and then repeat to yourself the above words as you do the actions.

For many people it takes trust and overcoming fear to move and act without using the familiar patterns of tension and misbalance. However, if you succeed in doing so a few times, the immediate rewards you experience will help you gain confidence with the new coordination. The process takes only a moment to use—as long as it takes to Pause. Using this process doesn't interfere with your work. Rather, it enhances your performance.

You can play a little game to begin increasing your effectiveness right now. Every time the phone rings, instead of answering it on the first or second ring, wait. Use your Awareness to notice if your neck begins to tighten as you reach to answer. Pause and Command your Advantage. Let your head and neck be free as you answer the phone. That's all it takes. The total time that process required was about 3 seconds. In these few moments, habit in your Primary control is changed from Risk to Advantage.

It is not how many minutes a day you can hold yourself correctly that creates a beneficial change. It is how many moments a day you can Pause to interrupt habit and restore your Advantage coordination that leads to a continuous beneficial Awareness. The process is brief and simple:

- Remember to be aware of your risky coordination
- Pause
- Visualize your Advantage coordination
- Leave your neck and head free

This whole process takes a moment. The more you use it, the more fluent you will become with it.

Although moving the head forward and up appears simple enough, it is easier said than done. The next chapter will introduce some procedures that will guide you into recognizing and correctly establishing the basic coordination that is your Advantage.

CHAPTER 5

Command Your *Advantage*

Now that you have a basic understanding of the Tools for Change, you may put them into action to Command your Advantage.

Your Advantage is a combination of accurate Awareness and healthy coordination of your Primary Control. Your goal is to have this Awareness and well coordinated Primary Control at your command, fluently and naturally.

Webster's New World Dictionary defines "*command*" as "1. to give an order or orders; to direct with authority; 2. to have authority or jurisdiction over; control." To really take control of your well being and your performance at work, you need to take control of how you are using your body. In this chapter, you will learn how to establish a healthy Primary Control through lying down, sitting, standing and walking. You will also learn the quality of muscle tone that allows your coordination to be free instead of stiff.

The Semi-Supine Position

This procedure is an important building block to improve your Primary Control coordination and Awareness. It affords you the opportunity to realize that lengthening your spine and widening your back are the result of releasing patterns of tension. Remember you are learning to stop doing something to achieve balance and ease. Take your time and enjoy discovering its benefits. What you learn and establish here will carry over to other procedures.

There are many immediate benefits you receive through this lying down procedure. Among them are:

- You easily learn a healthy relationship of the head, neck, and back without having to deal with the complexities of movement.
- You discover how to release tension in the muscles of your neck, shoulders and spine.
- The force of gravity as you are lying down helps to alleviate the extra curves of your spine, allowing the spine to return to its greatest possible length. As the vertebrae relax and ease away from each other, the discs are able to expand to their fullest potential.
- In relaxation, your nervous system has the chance to be reeducated.
- As you release tensions, you refresh yourself and regain poise.

Semi-supine position

Lying down is different than standing and sitting. Gravity has a different effect on your spine as you lie down. It can be easier to release tension in your neck and back. The resulting sensation will be different than standing, sitting, walking or bending.

Setting Up

To prepare for this procedure, you need a stack of paperback books that is about two and a half inches in thickness. The books placed under your head help you learn what it is like for the neck muscles to lengthen. It is best to do this procedure on a carpeted floor, so that you are on a comfortable but firm surface. Avoid using a bed for this process; most beds are too soft to support the correct relationship of your head, neck and spine.

The Lying Down Procedure

Lie down with your head resting on the books. Make sure that your neck is not in contact with the books; only your skull, the back of your head, should be resting on them. The stack of books should be high enough so that your head is not tipping back, but not so high that you have tension in the back of your neck and your throat feels cramped in front.

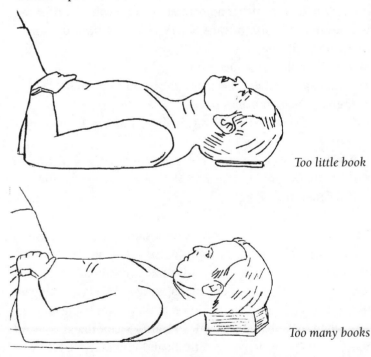

Too little book

Too many books

Leave your neck at ease while you bring each leg up, one at a time, to a bent position. Place your foot flat on the floor with your knee pointing to the ceiling. When both knees are up in this position, your feet should be approximately hip-width apart, and your knees should be directly over your big toe and second toe.

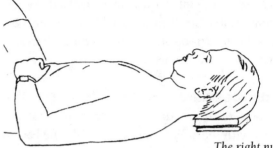

The right number of books

Your hands can be resting palm down on your torso, or your arms can be stretched out straight at your sides with your palms down on the floor.

Do not make any further adjustments when you first lie down. This is an opportunity to learn where you have built up tension during your active day.

Answer the following questions:

- Does your head pull back and down into the book?
- Are your neck muscles tense?
- Does one shoulder blade hit the floor differently than the other?
- Is your lower back tense or is it spreading wide on the floor?
- Do you feel more of one side of your pelvis against the floor than the other?
- Are your knees over your first and second toe?

After you have become aware of any tension and mis-balance you may have been carrying, put your Tools for Change to use. First, Pause and then Command your Advantage coordination.

In most other procedures or actions, we use "Head balancing forward and Up" in the directions. However this is confusing for many people when they are lying down. To learn to Command your Advantage in this position you can think and visualize the following Directions. Repeat the words in bold to yourself, verbatim and in order, while visualizing the subtle action.

- **Neck Free.** Visualize letting the muscles and vertebra of your neck ease back toward the floor with the pull of gravity. This is what neck free means.

- **Two ends of the spine easing away from each other.** As your neck becomes free, visualize your tailbone and your head gently moving in opposite Directions from each other.
- **Back spreading wide to breathe.** As your spine eases in both directions, visualize your back softening so it can spread wide into the floor surface. Then, allow breathing in without effort.

Repeat this sequence of phrases to yourself several times while visualizing the effect of the directions on your body. When you think and visualize the directions simultaneously, the benefits are strongest. It is important to stay awake during this procedure in order to maintain continuous Awareness as you develop your Advantage. You will undoubtedly notice that each time you stop focusing on these Directions, your body returns to its customary tensions and misbalance. Gently apply your Tools for Change by again becoming Aware, Pausing and Commanding Your Advantage. Be sure your head is not pulling back and down and that your knees remain hip-width apart and balanced directly over your big toe and second toe. The more you use this procedure, the more your tensions will continue to decrease.

The Button

This procedure will help you learn exactly what it means to send your head forward and up and release tension at the same time. The effect is similar to the previous procedure, but the process is different because gravity has a different pull on your head and spine when you are vertical rather than lying down horizontal.

You need a chair for this procedure. The best would be an office chair with a fairly firm, flat seat bottom and firm, flat seat back that does not recline much. The next best option would be a dining room type chair with those same qualities. Avoid molded plastic chairs, stuffed easy chairs and folding chairs.

Sit in the chair so that your buttocks are all the way back and your back is in contact with the back of the chair. Your feet should be flat on the floor.

- If you are wearing a shirt or blouse, look down at the second or third button from the top. (If you're dressed differently, imagine a button.) Return your head to an upright position, and then repeat the procedure. This time notice if both your neck and head move down toward the button. In looking down, it is very common for people to pull the neck forward and the head down.
- Now Pause and choose to look at the same button in a different way. This time move the neck back and lift the back of the head up and away from the button. In this movement, you are rotating the head forward at the top of the spine in order to look at the button.

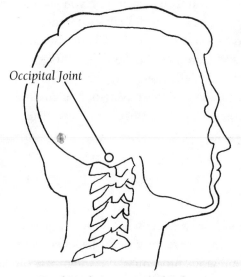

Occipital Joint

Head-Neck Anatomy and Balance

Locating the Head-Neck Joint

If you have done this procedure correctly, you have located the movable joint where the top of the spine meets the skull. This is called the occipital joint, and it is a key to moving with your Advantage. Because this joint is where the skull and vertebrae of the neck meet, we also call it the head-neck joint. In the illustration, you can see that the head-neck joint (occipital joint) is located just below the ear canal. We like to suggest to our students to think of this joint as right between the ears to make it easier to picture and to encourage a more upward direction of the head. Most of the weight of your head is forward of this joint.

Moving only your head, let gravity tip your head forward at this joint. You will notice that your chin drops slightly while the back of your head eases up. Do this several times until you can easily recognize the movement at the joint.

- Now look down again at the second or third button on your shirt or blouse. Notice what it feels like to rotate your head forward using the atlanto occipital joint.
- Notice the feeling of your spine lengthening and chest widening.

With few exceptions, new students can manage to do this movement successfully. Now try the next steps in order to advance your ability to apply this forward and up coordination.

- Choose a point directly across the room to focus on. Keeping your eyes on this point, again rotate your head forward, as above. Repeat this movement several times, reducing the forward rotation so that it is slight but definitely present.
- Now keeping the movement connected to the head-neck joint, turn your head to one side and then to the other.

Because this movement might be unfamiliar, you may at first notice some tension in the muscles in the front and back of your neck, almost like holding it in traction. In order to release this tension, it is important to learn how to control the quality of muscle tone in that area. Remain seated in your chair as you do the following procedure.

- Think to yourself the words "Neck Free." Continue to hold this thought as you proceed.
- Release the muscles of your abdomen to let the breath come in. Repeat this several times without hurry.
- Now release your buttocks to spread wide. Then simultaneously release your abdomen and your buttocks to let your breath in. Continue holding the thought of "neck free."
- Let your entire back lean into the chair and spread wide to let the breath in. This feeling of the back releasing is similar to what you learned in the semi-supine procedure.

- Now put them all together. With neck free, release your abdomen, buttocks and back to let your breath come in. Repeat this several times.

It is important not to force an expanded breath. Use the release just before inhaling. Besides enabling your muscles to relax, another positive effect of this process is a freer, more expanded breath. Eventually, whether you are breathing in or out, you will be able to release tension in your muscles. When your Primary Control is efficient, your respiration is also more efficient.

This procedure has combined thinking and visualizing, controlled balance and muscular release. As you practice this, you will notice that the beneficial effects are strongest when you both think and visualize the process as you do it. Without Awareness, old patterns of tension and misbalance return. You can use your Awareness of the contrast between old habits and your beneficial Advantage as a tool to help you change.

Standing

Many jobs require a great deal of standing without much movement. Standing in a misbalanced way is a constant strain on the musculature and skeletal system and causes unnecessary fatigue and pain. The following procedures will help you apply your Advantage to standing.

To build your Awareness, observe yourself in a mirror or have a friend give you feedback or make a video of you to help you identify what you are doing.

To begin, use the plumb line procedure. Stand sideways in front of a full-length mirror. Now imagine a vertical line passing through your body from above your head and going down through the middle of your ankles. Now observe yourself carefully.
- Is your head forward of the plumb line?
- Are your shoulders forward or behind the plumb line?
- Is your upper back behind the plumb line?
- Is your pelvis forward of the plumb line?
- Are your knees forward or behind the plumb line?

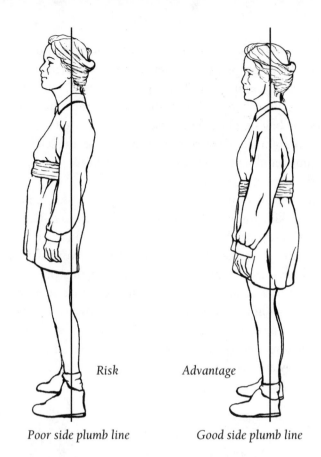

Risk   Advantage

Poor side plumb line   *Good side plumb line*

Notice any tension you may feel in your body. Many people habitually stand with their ears and pelvis forward of the plumb line and their shoulders too far behind it. The long term impact of standing with this misbalanced position is constant repeated strain on the whole back and legs, resulting in damage to muscles, tendons and joints.

Now apply your Advantage to standing. Let your head lead forward and up. Looking down at "the button," let the spine follow the head up. Now check your body's profile in the mirror again. Where are you in relation to the plumb line now? You may recall how faulty sensory Awareness can mislead you to feel in balance when you are not and off-balance when you are perfectly aligned. That is why you need visual feedback when you first begin applying your Advantage to standing.

The plumb line can also be used with a front view of the torso. Facing the mirror, picture the vertical line passing through your nose, breast bone and pubic bone. If you are collapsing or twisting your spine, your body will not line up with the plumb line. (See illustration below) Observe yourself.

- Is the right shoulder higher or lower than the left?
- Is one hand hanging lower than the other?
- Does your head tilt to one side?

Apply your Advantage and then check yourself again in the mirror. In checking for tension in your body, be sure to notice whether your knees are locked into a stiff, straight position or a tensed, bent position. Let your knees be loose and at ease. Avoid standing still for long periods of time while working on this process. Move around and then come back to standing. Command your Advantage and then check to see how accurate your Awareness is by again observing your image or reflection. It takes repeated and persistent attention to reeducate Awareness, but the payoff is in less tension, more energy and less wear on your structure.

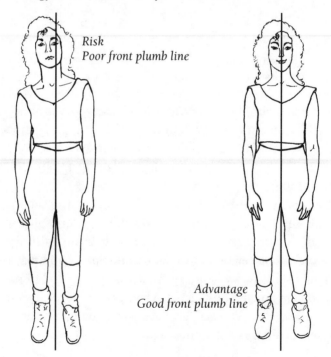

Risk
Poor front plumb line

Advantage
Good front plumb line

Walking

When the foot steps forward and takes the weight of the body, the Primary Control is what leads the body and determines the quality of the movement. When walking, many people have their head pull down toward their feet, creating a compression in the spine, hips, knees, ankles and feet and requiring more energy than needed. In the well-coordinated walk, the head moves forward and up to lead movement which pulls the spine up and reduces the amount of tension needed to complete the movement.

In doing this process, it will be very helpful to observe yourself. A video tape would be best, but a mirror is some help. Start out by walking with your normal stride to observe what that is like.

- As you take a step, do your head and neck pull down toward the foot that is leading?
- Does this pulling down happen with one foot more than with the other?
- Does the weight of your body feel as if it is going down as you step forward?
- Does your head move from side to side as you walk?
- Does your upper body lean back as your foot steps out in front?
- Do your ankles and feet stiffen as you place your foot down with each step?
- When you walk faster, do your neck and shoulders tighten?

There is a great deal to observe in walking, so it is best to take your time and review these questions over the course of a few days. When you feel familiar with your normal way of walking, find an open space to walk in where you can begin to apply your Advantage. Start by standing with your Advantage, recalling all you learned in the previous exercise. Take time to be as clear with this as possible. The most important movement as you begin to walk is for your head to lead forward and up.

- As your head initiates the first step, allow the Advantage balance you established in standing to continue. Leave

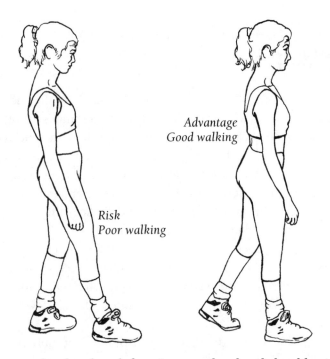

Advantage
Good walking

Risk
Poor walking

your head and neck free. Let your head and shoulders
release away from each other.

- With each step, renew your commitment to let the head
  lead and the body follow. Leaving your head and neck free,
  direct your head to lead forward and up. Very often when
  learning something new the tendency is to hold your
  breath. Remember to breathe.

If you have been used to walking with your shoulders and upper
back behind your plumb line, this new coordination might feel as if
you are inclining forward. Observe yourself in a mirror or on a video
in order to prove to yourself that you are upright, so that you can be
inspired to develop your Advantage. That old way of walking with
backward balance generally is accompanied by forward movement
with stiff feet and legs. This coordination is stressful to the body and
can cause fatigue for your back, particularly the lower back.

When your head leads forward and up to walk, at first you may
feel like you are going up, up, up, or as if you are falling forward.
Just continue to move with the head easing up, noting what hap-

pens as you observe yourself walking. In a very short time, this new coordination will feel normal and balanced.

About 95% of our students start to laugh the first time they follow our guidance to walk with their head leading with ease and balance. They think they must look preposterous to us. Actually, they look graceful, and as they become accustomed to their new coordination, they notice that they feel light and springy.

Some people have an entrenched habit of moving the head from side to side. If you find yourself doing this, try the following:

- Start with your Advantage in standing. Focus on an object at eye level, across the room or some distance away. While continuing to look at the object, think to yourself, "Eyes wide," and activate your peripheral vision to take in other objects in the room or the area. Sustaining this quality of seeing, visualize a line extending from your eyes to your chosen object.
- With your neck free, let your head lead you along this line as your body follows. Do not let your head move sideways or up and down.

Repeat this numerous times in order to develop your Awareness and your skill.

Walking Game

At first this new coordination of walking may seem to you unnatural or conspicuous. Don't let your old faulty Awareness prevent you from continuing to develop your Advantage. To help you along, here is a simple game you can play.

- Find a place where you can walk for a continuous distance, like a corridor or outdoors.
- Starting by Commanding your Advantage, walk for 8 to 12 steps.
- Continuing to walk, revert to your old coordination of walking for the next 8 to 12 steps.
- Now, without stopping, Command your Advantage again and walk the next 8 to 12 steps.

- Continue alternating between these two as you walk. In doing this procedure, you may notice how much more easeful walking with your Advantage is compared to your normal walk. As you practice, you develop your Awareness and the ability to make the choice to Command your Advantage in walking.

Return to these procedures from time to time—weeks, months and even years from now. Let these procedures be guides to improvement and learning. They will carry over into daily movement. You can always keep improving your walk by fine-tuning your Awareness. Now that you have applied your Advantage to the basic movements and use of the body, we will move on in the next three chapters to applying your Advantage in specific work circumstances. Each chapter will present procedures related to different types of jobs, but all are built upon what you have learned in this chapter.

CHAPTER 6

Working at the Desk and Keyboard

People who spend a great deal of time working at desks regularly come to us for help because they are experiencing pain in their hands, arms, shoulders or necks. The advancement of technology has meant that those who work in offices are increasingly required to do small repetitive movements. Limited and repeated movements when combined with other stresses and strains can put office workers at Risk and lead to Repetitive Strain Injuries.

A number of elements combine to create your Advantage in the office. While they may include environmental factors such as high quality monitors, keyboards and chairs, the real key to preventing RSI's lies in how the body is used in relation to its surroundings. In this chapter, we will present procedures that will help you to develop your Advantage while sitting and working at your desk, using a computer keyboard, reaching out for objects, and talking on the telephone. As you learn these procedures, continue to apply your Tools for change with your Primary Control—Awareness, Pause to interrupt habit and Direction (visualizing your Advantage).

When we ask our clients in their first session whether or not they are using a good office chair to sit in while working, more often than not they answer yes. If they say no or are not sure, we guide them first to select a decent chair, and from there we work on developing new habits in using it. Too often we have seen that while people usually remark about how much more comfortable they are in chairs that adjust for better support, the problem with their hands, arms, shoulders and neck persists until they learn coordination and ease while sitting. As you recall from the example in Chapter 1 of the insurance company worker slumping in her chair, the best chair does not guarantee that the causes RSI's will be eliminated. However, how you use that chair can make all the difference you need.

With few exceptions, the people who come to us for help are stuck in faulty sensory Awareness; over the course of years, tension and misbalance have come to feel right to them. In this case, using a new chair can, in fact, cause even more problems, especially if the instruction they receive in how to sit in it lacks understanding of coordination and kinesthetic learning. Carolyn was referred to Alexander Technique by her doctor due to painful spasms in her

What Makes a Good Chair?

- A firm, wide, padded seat that adjusts to tilt forward and back is recommended. Your legs should be comfortably bent so your feet touch the floor. There should be no feeling of sliding off the chair. You should be able to easily detect the balance of your head, neck and back above your sit-bones.
- The back of the chair should be high enough and wide enough to feel your entire back against it. It should be adjustable to move forward and back. Some chairs have adjustments that increase lumbar support for people who need it. These can enhance the benefits gained from a good chair.
- The chair should have a quick and easy adjustment for height to facilitate changes for various tasks, or to readily adjust for different people who use the same chair.
- For people that need to turn to work in different positions at their work station the chair should easily swivel and roll. Be sure to get castors that are meant to work on the type of floor surface in your work environment.

back and shoulders which started on the day her new office chair was delivered. She explained that the person who delivered the chair instructed her to hold herself up straight and demonstrated what that meant. Carolyn tried to follow these instructions throughout the rest of the day. The next morning she ended up at the doctor with disabling pain. Coordinating balance and ease while sitting is equally if not more important than the chair. To avoid Risk, you need to know what the Advantage coordination and balance is for yourself.

Sitting with Your Advantage

When you sit, do you:

- try to straighten your back but find that you are tensing and arching it instead?
- get neck, shoulder and back tension occasionally, frequently or constantly?
- collapse when you need to relax?
- "pull down" in your Primary Control?

To develop your Advantage, it is helpful to begin by recognizing if you are at Risk when you are sitting at your desk, attending meetings, or working at the file cabinet.

The most typical error of sitting is to misbalance the head, neck and spine as shown in the illustration. This misbalance creates a downward pressure on the spine. Notice that the subject is rounding her back in the typical "poor posture slump." This can eventually cause a distinct hump to develop in the upper back and shoulder area as the overworked muscles of the upper back become bulky and congested. Observe in the illus-

Slumping

tration how the upper back is rounded backward. This creates a rounding of the lower spine that puts the lower back, hips and legs at risk of injury.

Another common pattern of risk in sitting is to arch in front of the sit bones.

A common error of "good posture" is the attempt to sit up straight by arching your back with excessive strain. Observe how the figure in the illustration below holds the spine up by lifting the chest up and out. This posture, commonly known as swayback, automatically causes the lower back to overwork. Curving the upper back too far forward creates tension in the shoulder blades, which are pulling in towards the spine. These misbalances create fatigue in the neck, shoulders and back muscles and can be the beginning of many RSI's.

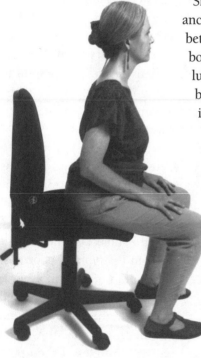

Sitting comfortably and with balance depends upon the relationship between your head, neck, spine, sit bones, and legs. In the following illustration, note how the spine is balanced vertically, and the head is balanced on top of the spine. This continuously releases tension from the neck and spine.

Arching Forward

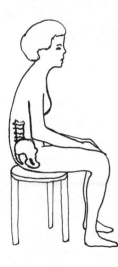

Whether you sit with ease and balance, or with a harmful strained position depends on the coordination of your Primary Control and your Awareness of it. Ease and balance is achieved when you prevent the compression of rounding or arching your spinal column.

Note in the illustration of *Ease and Balance*, that the head balances forward and upward at the top of the spine. Through this the spine is lengthened and the back is widened.

Ease and Balance

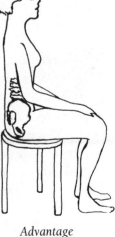
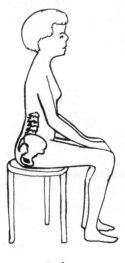

Risk
Rounding

Risk
Arching

Advantage
Lengthening

Sitting Procedure

In the following procedure, you will learn to develop ease and balance in your Primary Control while sitting in your office chair. To follow this guidance accurately, you need a good office chair or a chair with a firm flat seat bottom, such as a wooden dining room chair. Use a camera or a mirror, or enlist the help of a friend, to help you verify what is happening with your balance. Recall what you have learned in Chapter 5 about the location of your head-neck joint (p.74), and keep it in mind throughout this procedure.

- Sit on the front edge of the chair, without leaning against the back. Place your feet flat on the floor.
- Begin by locating your sit-bones. These bones, the ischial tuberosities, are actually at the bottom of your pelvis. To locate them, slide both your hands, with the palms up, under your buttocks so that you feel the sit-bones pressing against your fingers. You can think of the sit bones as the little feet on which the spine balances.
- Command your Advantage. Locating your head-neck joint, balance your head so that the sit-bones are in a plumb line under the ears. Remain sitting on your hands during the rest of this procedure.
- Contrast your risk. Let your back round into a slump. Feel the pelvis tip back and your lower spine extend back behind the sit bones. Notice where your pelvis is now in relation to your fingers. Where is your body weight in relation to your sit bones? This is risk.
- Arch your back forward as far as you can. Feel the pelvis tip forward, almost lifting up off your fingers. Notice where your body weight is now. This is also risk.
- Tip your pelvis back until you feel your sit bones pressing down into your fingers. Let your pelvis and lower spine move back until your sit bones are pressing directly down onto your fingers with the most force. This force is your body weight evenly balanced on your sit-bones. This is your Advantage while sitting.

- Staying with this balance, again Command your Advantage. Again, locate your head-neck joint and balance your head so that the sit-bones are in a plumb line under the ears.
- Repeat these sitting positions of Risk and Advantage.
- Rounding and compressing the spine back.
- Arching and tightening the spine forward.
- Balancing and lengthening over the sit bones.

Take note that the pelvis can tip forward or back, and its position affects whether or not the spine is balanced under the head.

- Remove your hands from under your buttocks by gently sliding them out sideways.
- Repeat the three balances now without your fingers as a guide. Sense the rocking of the pelvis, the movement in the spine, and the shift in body weight.
- Take a moment to appreciate this middle balance. Allow your buttocks and legs to release tension while maintaining the balance of your head, neck, spine and pelvis. You needn't tighten your legs to hold yourself up. When sitting, your head and spine can balance on top of the sit-bones without tension in the legs.
- Command your Advantage again. While breathing quietly, observe the entire rib cage expanding and collapsing. Don't make the ribs move with a deliberate big breath. Rather, just observe that they are unobstructed in being able to expand and collapse in quiet breathing. Visualize this process as you are doing it. Observing your breathing in this way can help to maintain a comfortable balance in your torso and neck.
- To complete this process, put everything together:
- Command your Advantage.
- Appreciate the balance of your spine and body weight directly over your sit-bones.
- Observe that your ribs are unobstructed as they expand and collapse in quiet breathing.

As you repeat these procedures, you will continue to grow more and more familiar with your support and balance and ease.

If you sit for extended periods in your job, it is important to give yourself a break from one continuous position. Find different positions in which you can use your Advantage in a well coordinated manner. You can become comfortable with different leg positions. Sometimes you can have your legs spread wide apart sitting up on the front edge of your chair or sitting back in the chair. The same applies with leaving your legs together. The change is good. Occasionally sit all the way back in your chair and let your back lengthen and widen into the back surface similar to the sensation of the Lying Semi-Supine procedure. This should be accomplished comfortably without rounding.

Procedure for Bending from the Hip

Now that you are familiar with your Advantage in sitting, you can learn to carry this into other activities at your desk. Notice what happens as you lean forward to reach for something. Do you bend at the hips or do you round your back and bend your spine? Or do you arch your back and create excessive tension in your hips, making it difficult for them to move? Either one of these leads to compression of your spine, resulting in weakness and fatigue, and putting you at Risk or causing severe RSI's. In the following procedure you will learn to apply your Advantage by bending from the hips to move in your chair. Sit in your chair, according to the guidance in the previous section.

- Command your Advantage, letting your head ease forward and upward. Let your spine follow and lengthen as you rock forward. If you notice any tension in your legs, release it to let your hip joints move easily. It's important to avoid the mistake of arching your back as you rock forward to an inclined position. Let your head lead your spine to lengthen, preventing the spine from rounding or arching. Allow the movement to take place at your hips while your back remains relaxed.

- Rock back to an upright position, letting your head continue to lead your spine to lengthen. Ease back to balance directly above your sit bones. Again, use your attention to prevent the spine from rounding or arching while the movement takes place at your hips.
- Gently and slowly repeat this movement, rocking forward and backward several times. Observe how much tension in your pelvis and legs you are able to release from start to finish of the complete rocking movement. Continue to Command your Advantage as you practice this procedure.

As you have seen, even the best office equipment can't solve problems caused by misuse of the body. Learning how to sit at your desk with your Advantage is the key to preventing RSI's from developing. The bonus is that, as you develop your Advantage, you will find that you are conserving your energy during your working hours and returning home with energy to spare.

Applying Your Advantage to Looking Down at the Keyboard or Work Surface

For John, sitting was not the only area of Risk at work. He spends up to six hours a day bent over a computer keyboard. When he came to learn Alexander Technique, John had been experiencing the second stage of Repetitive Strain Injury—sometimes waking-up a little stiff, and then the stiffness turning into pain over the course of the day. Together we discovered that whenever he looked down at his keyboard, he bent his head using the vertebrae from his mid-neck rather than from the head-neck joint.

Developing the new and healthy habit of looking down by rotating his head at this joint has required added attention. Especially when John gets engrossed in his work, he has to Pause and remind himself to Command his Advantage and again think of his head-neck joint as between his ears before looking down. Making this effort, however, has alleviated his pain and undoubtedly prevented the development of a serious Repetitive Strain Injury.

Like John, many people bend in the neck and in the upper back to look down at a keyboard or at a work surface. This means that your head is pulling down and the muscles in your neck tensing. As we have seen, tension in the neck affects the entire body.

Risk
Pulling Down to See

Advantage
Forward and Up to See

In the above left illustration, notice how the figure looks down by bending from the middle of her neck and upper back. Consequently, her chest is sunken and collapsed. This restricts breathing, compresses the spine and promotes harmful strain throughout the shoulders and arms. Notice what happens as you look down. Is your head moving at your head-neck joint while your neck and spine lengthen? Or are you pulling your head and neck down with your back rounding? Pulling down with rounding is the most common Risky coordination for working at a desk. This imbalance is the cause of most RSI's in the neck, shoulders, back, arms and even in the wrists.

If you wear glasses, you probably encounter an additional concern. You may be use to holding your head in a certain position in order to see through your glasses properly. Especially if you have bifocals, you might be in the habit of tilting your head back in order to see when you are working on a surface. Over time, the vision adapts to the misbalance. So when the head goes forward and up in developing your Advantage, you may notice immediately that your range of vision "feels" different. Stick with it, and you will succeed to leave your neck and head in a comfortable balance while seeing with your glasses. If you must move your head to utlize your bifocals or trifocals, pause to free your neck to do so.

Whether you are working at a keyboard or doing other work that requires you to look down at a surface, to eliminate risk it is important that you allow your head to balance forward and up at the occipital joint.

Procedure for Looking Down

Begin the following procedure by reviewing your skills for sitting in a chair with your Advantage.

- Locate your head-neck joint. (See page 74 if you want to review this.) With your neck free of tension, look down only with your eyes.
- Allow your head to rock forward gently at the head-neck joint only. The front of the head is heavier than the back, so you can let gravity cause the front to tip forward. The neck does not bend in this movement. Without holding the neck in a stiff position, make sure it does not pull forward and down.

Repeat this process two or three times with Awareness.

- Is your head rocking forward at the head-neck joint or at the mid-neck?
- Are your neck and head pulling downward?
- With your head still balanced forward at the head-neck joint, Command your Advantage, visualizing the head leading the spine to lengthen.

When your Advantage is at work, the head, balanced on top of the spine, rotates forward and up on the head-neck joint. This allows your back and chest to stay wide. Repeat these instructions several times a day as you become familiar with this new manner of moving your head.

Raising Your Hands to the Keyboard

Using your hands at the keyboard and desk with excessive tension can lead to carpal tunnel syndrome and tendinitis in the arms, wrists and shoulders. Although the symptoms occur in the arms, the problem stems from the relationship between the head, neck and spine. Tension and misbalance in the neck and head puts pressure on the nerves that extend down the arms and hands.

In the illustration below, you can see that the neck is thrust forward and the shoulders are rounded forward. This strain on the neck and back muscles causes excess tension in the biceps, elbows, wrists and hands. This pattern of tension starts right at the point when the hands are lifted up to use them, and it intensifies as work continues. Once you have had an experience of using the arms and wrists without tension, you will begin to notice the difference. Learning some basic anatomy of the arms and hands is essential to beginning to use them without strain.

Pulling Downward to Use the Arms

Anatomy of the Arms and Hands
Where exactly is the first joint of the arm?

This joint is located where the collar bone meets the breast bone—the sternoclavicular joint. Most of our students don't realize that there is a joint here and are surprised to discover that the collar bone is actually supposed to move.

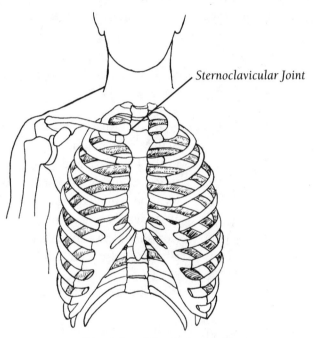

First Joint of the Arm

Place the fingers of your left hand on your right collar bone midway between your breast bone and shoulder, then move your right shoulder up, down and all around. It really does move! The outer end of the collar bone forms a bony protective shelf over the shoulder joint, which is the second arm joint.

Where exactly is the shoulder?

When we ask people who come to us with shoulder pain to point out where their shouder joint is, almost without fail, they indicate the front of their shoulder area somewhere along the collar bone. When we ask them to reach for an object in front of them, they move their arms by tightening their neck and shoulder as they pull the shoulder forward and up towards the neck. We kindly inform them at that point that they are suffering from a "mislocated" shoulder joint.

As the following illustration shows, the shoulder joint actually is located in the back outside portion of the shoulder girdle. The upper arm bone forms a joint with the shoulder blade.

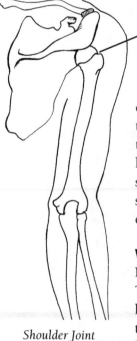

Shoulder Joint

While visualizing the actual location of the shoulder joint, move your arms up to the keyboard and back down several times. Continue to visualize this joint's location while typing as well. When the shoulder joint is correctly located, tension should be minimal as you bend your elbow to raise your hands.

Where exactly is the elbow joint?
Many of the people who learn Alexander Technique with us are surprised to clearly locate where the actual joint movement of the elbow takes place. They point at the bony point that sticks out when the elbow

Shoulder Joint

is bent to first identify the joint's location. We help them to discover that there are two bones of the forearm (radius and ulna) that form a joint with the upper arm bone (humerus). These three bones join together to create a union of the forearm and upper arm that allows the forearm to bend and extend as well as rotate from the upper arm. Look at the following illustration and bend your own elbow and carefully realize the correct location of the moving elbow joint.

For people who suffer with tendinitis in the elbow or other forearm and wrist problems, this is invaluable information. Too often these people hold their elbow stiff, as part of a faulty pattern of tension in their daily routine. When they change the habit, the problems disappear.

Where is the Wrist Joint?

Many of our students make the mistake of thinking their wrist joint is located at the bumps that can be felt close to where a wrist watch is worn. Actually, the joint is closer to where the palm begins. Carefully study the illustration of the wrist anatomy and feel your own wrists as you move them around.

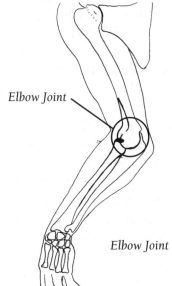

Elbow Joint

Elbow Joint

Once you accurately locate your elbow and wrist joints, pay attention to your daily movements to discover if you are letting them move appropriately or not. Too many of our students are amazed at how strange correct movements feel, until they can Pause to use them regularly.

Wrist Joint

Wrist Joint

Freeing the Forearms and Wrists

Office work often requires people to use their wrists either in one position or with a limited range of movement. The wrists, however, have a broad range of movement—up and down, sideways, rotation. To keep the muscles and joints free of Risk, it is important to use this full range. Move your wrists sideways and around. Repeat these movements a few times to help you understand free flexion and extension of your wrists and your wrist's range of movement.

Two important movements are largely unused by people who suffer with tendinitis in the elbow or other forearm and wrist problems.

1) Free forearm and wrist rotation.

2) Free wrist flexion and extension.

Too often these people also hold their elbows stiff, as part of a faulty pattern of tension in their daily routine. When they change, the problems disappear.

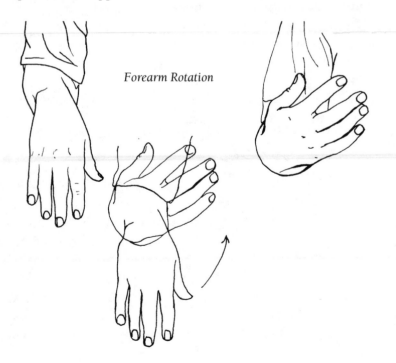

Forearm Rotation

The forearm is made up of two bones—the radius and the ulna. The radius is the bone on the side of the thumb and the ulna is the bone on the side of the pinky. Hand, wrist and elbow movement depend upon these two bones. Risk occurs when the radius is restricted by tension and not allowed to move freely.

Hold the left forearm with your right hand as you turn your left palm to face up and then down. You should be able to feel the radius bone (thumb side) rotating around the ulna (pinky finger side). If it does not, you may be recognizing some risk in your arm movement.

At first easy rotation of the hand from side to side, as shown in the above illustration, was an alien feeling for most people who have come to see us with painful symptoms in their arms and shoulders.

The other movement that goes largely unused during the day is free wrist flexion. Too many of the people who come in to see us are keeping the shoulders, elbows and wrists in stiff positions. We often have to repeatedly direct them to release the stiff holding of their arms along with their stiff necks.

The reason these two types of movements do not readily occur is that they are restricted by muscular tension from doing so.

Dangerous Positions for the Wrists at the Keyboard or Mouse

Not only do many office workers hold excess tension in their arms when they use the computer keyboard and mouse, they also hold them in positions that can accelerate injury to their elbows and wrists. It is important to point out that these dangers apply to musical keyboardists as well. The first position to beware of is pulling the wrist to the outside creating a straight line extending down the radius bone and thumb.

Other dangerous injuries can occur if the wrists are held in a straight position or overly flexed position. Wrist rests can actually encourage over straightening the wrists with excess tension when the resting surface is too low. We have seen many people pushing their wrists down into the rests with tension accompanied by a pulling down in their necks. Even with wrist rests at a more ideal height, many people are unknowingly forcing their wrists down onto them with tension. When people place their wrist on a wrist rest when using a mouse, they move only the hand while the rest of their arm is still. This causes the arm to become stiff and fixed. This is all very risky.

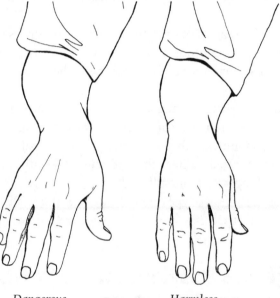

Dangerous   Harmless

Your Advantage at the keyboard or when using a mouse will not depend on any device that claims to support your body in a correct position. It depends on your well-coordinated Primary Control and freedom in movement, especially when your job requires you to do small repetitive movements.

a) Poor Use of Wrists: Risk

b) Poor Use of Wrists: Risk

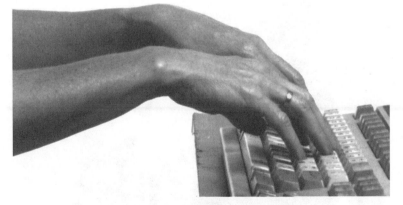

c) Good Use of Wrists: Advantage

Procedure for Raising Your Hands to the Keyboard

By introducing these procedures into your work at the keyboard, you will learn free and easy use of the arms. Begin by using the skills you have acquired for sitting with your Advantage at your work area.

- Command your Advantage. As your head leads forward and up, let your arms hang loose at your sides. Think of them as being supported by the spine as they hang from your shoulder joints.
- With your elbows continuing to hang freely from the shoulder joints, let your wrists and hands begin to rise. Avoid any tension in your shoulders or biceps. Allow loose, easy movement in the flexion and rotation of your wrists and forearms as you accomplish this slight movement. Allow the elbows to hang free. If someone were to bump your elbows, they should swing freely like a pendulum.
- Move your head forward and up as you place your hands on the keyboard.

Advantage
Head Easing Forward and Up to Type

Most keyboard entries can be made with free and hanging elbows. As you move your fingers on the keys, maintain ease and freedom in your hands and wrists. The movement of wrists and fingers should be light and easy. Very small shifts around the keyboard can allow movement in all of the joints. When you reach forward, allow your elbows to move with a sense of the back of the arms being involved rather than the biceps. Let the back widen as you reach. Avoid letting your head and neck pull down to see what your hands are doing. Continue sending your head up and away from your hands as you let your head balance easily at your head-neck joint. Repeat these instructions many times to become familiar with easy and safe arm movements.

Using the Telephone with Your Advantage

Talking on the phone regularly as part of your business routine can be a literal pain in the neck. This pain can also extend into the shoulder, arms and hands. People commonly hold the phone with their shoulder while writing, or doing other things. Even without this hazard, many people pull their head and neck down while they tighten their shoulder up, holding the phone with their hand. Unless you get a headset phone to free up your hands, it is important to learn a way to use the phone that eliminates the stress and risk of RSI's.

- Do you find yourself always holding the phone up to one side of your head?
- Do you cradle the phone between your shoulder and head so you can use both your hands to do something?
- Do you bring your head down to the phone to talk?

Notice in the illustration on the following page how the figure is pulling down to one side to meet the phone. His shoulder is tensing to hold the phone. This tension is broadcast down the arms and into the wrists and hands. As he leans forward to use the phone, the pulling down of his head and neck is intensified, thus creating

Risk: Common Errors of Using the Phone

rounding in his upper back. Safe, harmless use of the telephone depends on keeping your neck free while continuing to ease the head forward and upward without any tension throughout your shoulders and arms.

Procedure for Using the Phone

In this process you can combine all the skills you have acquired in the previous procedures for sitting, looking down, and using your arms with your Advantage. Begin by sitting in your chair with ease and balance.

- Pause before reaching to pick up the phone. At this point decide not to allow the harmful tension pattern to occur in your neck and shoulders.
- Command your Advantage by directing your head forward and up, both before and as you reach for the phone.

Advantage: Using the phone

- Bring the phone up to your ear, rather than letting the head come down to the phone. Avoid lifting your shoulder to hold the phone against your ear.
- As you talk, continue to direct your neck to be free and your head to move forward and upward.

Whether you are reaching to make a call or to answer one, successfully stopping a moment to Pause, become Aware and set your intention to use the phone with your Advantage will eliminate much stress from your day.

If you spend considerable time on the phone as part of your business routine, the type of phone you use can make your job much more comfortable and put you less at risk for developing RSI's. Regular phones, even with special cradling devices, are problematic because they present the opportunity for your neck and shoulders to tense if you use them to hold the phone in place. Try a headset for one or two weeks and you will not want to give it up. The next best alternative is a speaker phone. (When using a speakerphone, however, you might want to alert your party to the fact that his or her voice is being broadcast.)

It seems that a job in an office should be less risky than a job where you might be more physically active. However, the sedentary nature of working at a desk presents many hidden dangers as illustrated in this chapter. Learning how to apply your Advantage while sitting and working at a desk is essential for both your safety and wellbeing.

Driving a vehicle as part of your job or for commuting is equally sedentary and potentially risky. The next chapter, will help you identify risk and Advantage specific to the car, truck, bus or plane that you may find yourself in.

CHAPTER 7

The Driver

Albert the realtor, whom you may recall from Chapter 3 was diagnosed with a deteriorating disk in his neck after an extremely painful episode while driving. As he turned to look to the left before merging in traffic, pain had shot through his arms and neck. Albert's injury was not caused in that single instant of turning but had been developing over time as he used his body in a stressful way while driving. The basic coordination Albert had grown used to was one that was continually compressing his spine. This influenced the way he sat in his car, the way he turned to look around in traffic, and eventually caused the disk in his neck to deteriorate.

Unfortunately, the risk that caused Albert's injury is widespread among drivers and can manifest in many different ways—stress, low back pain, sciatica, shoulder and arm pain, and even heart and breathing problems. Some of the serious injuries that can occur from poor coordination in driving include cervical syndrome, herniated disks and sciatica.

Driving automobiles and trucks requires putting the body in positions that it was not designed to be in for extended periods. Many workers commute to work, driving one or more hours per day. Others, such as taxi drivers, truck drivers, police, and sales representatives, are subjected to these unnatural positions forty or more hours per week. Add to this the stresses of traffic delays, speeded up traffic patterns, hazardous weather, and fear of collision, and it is clear that driving poses a substantial risk for developing Repetitive Strain Injuries. While vehicle manufacturers are doing their best to design car and truck seats that make the driver more comfortable, the most important support you can have in driving is developing your Advantage. The design of the car seat cannot make up for risk you cause to yourself.

The first day we saw Albert, we began to recognize the cause of his injury. As he sat in the chair at our office, he was rounding and tightening forward from his upper back through his neck. When we asked him to point to the joint where his head moves at the top of his spine, he indicated the back of his neck between the base of his skull and his shoulders. When we asked him to point to his shoulder joint, he indicated the front of his shoulder area just above and to the inside of his armpit. As we have seen in the previous chapter, misunderstanding the location of these joints is connected with risk in moving the body. In addition, when we asked Albert to sit in the chair in a relaxed way, he collapsed even further into the rounding position. The twinge of pain Albert immediately experienced was proof that his understanding of a relaxed position was actually one that was compressing his spine. All of these errors in understanding how to use his body with balance and ease had ended up causing Albert's injury.

When you drive, do you:
- feel more stressed than usual?
- grip the wheel tightly?
- have difficulty getting in and out of the car?
- feel aches and pain after driving for more than an hour?
- develop headaches and shoulder tension?
- get an aching back?
- develop leg pain?

If you answer yes to any of these questions, learning how to apply your Advantage to sitting and moving while driving can begin to bring you immediate relief and, in the long run, help to prevent the dangers and pain of Repetitive Strain Injuries. In this chapter, we will consider aspects of what kind of seat in your vehicle can contribute to your support, but we will focus primarily on what you can do yourself to develop your Advantage while driving.

Features of a Supportive Seat in Your Vehicle

The drawbacks of a poorly designed seat in your vehicle can be difficult to overcome. If at all possible, drive in a seat that you can easily use with your Advantage. What you want to look for are certain qualities in the structure of your car seat.

The sitting surface needs to give you firm support, but not be so hard that your buttocks feel uncomfortable or "fall asleep." You also want to make sure that the rear of the seat does not slant down at an angle and cause your pelvis to tilt and your lower back to round, as illustrated below. This is a serious loss of the lumbar curve of your spine and represents a major Risk.

Rounding of the spine creates both tightening and overstretching of the muscles and can lead to an unstable back prone to pain and weakness. This risk can also lead to symptoms of sciatica .

The seatback should be fairly firm and for the most part flat. One that supports you in an upright rather than reclined position will be easiest to use with your Advantage. A firm, flat seat back can help you lengthen and widen your back. Unfortunately in too many cases, the part of the seatback that is supposed to support your low back starts to wear out and lose firmness after a relatively short time. This can be especially true in the case of law enforcement vehicles or taxis which are often used around the clock. Improper support in this area also allows your lower back to round. The middle and upper parts of the seat back can also wear out in a way that encourages risk.

In certain vehicles, such as sportscars and some sedans, the driver's legs primarily extend out from the seat rather than down toward the floor, as they would in sitting in a chair. This is an unnatural position to endure for prolonged and repeated periods.

The first step in establishing your Advantage while driving is to do everything possible to make sure your car seat is not causing problems. This may mean correcting the seat with support cushions (see page 158 in appendix B) or installing a new seat altogether. However, even this may not take care of the problem if you are unaware of habits that are putting you at risk.

Toni is a successful sales representative who routinely covers a large region every two weeks. Her daily routine includes stopping at about ten to fifteen accounts per day. By her fourth year on the job, recurring low back pain and sciatica had changed from occasional to almost constant. Toni bought a new car with seats she believed were more comfortable and supportive. After driving it for a couple of months, her pain had eased only slightly. Next she tried different types of cushions, beaded back rests, and a variety of other supports. Her pain became a little less constant but still serious, and some newer symptoms developed—neck and shoulder tension.

When Toni came to our office for the first time, we noticed that when she bent over to fill out a form, her lower back and pelvis rounded. The rounding continued up the spine so that she was bending forward from the middle of her back as her neck and head tightened forward as she wrote. When she sat up to talk with us, her pelvis and low back remained rounded, and although her upper spine straightened somewhat, her neck still strained forward, pulling her head with it. When we pointed these elements of tension and misbalance out to her, Toni remarked that she didn't feel tense or out of balance.

Faulty Awareness leading to poor head-neck coordination can cause a chain reaction of chronic conditions for a driver:

- Repetitive tightening in your neck and shoulders can wear discs and joint tissues in vertebrae and shoulder resulting in inflammation, disc damage in the neck (cervical vertebra), and pressure on nerves leading from neck to arms and hands.
- Continuous lack of support in the lower back can lead to aggravation of the sciatic nerve, and compression and deterioration of the lumbar discs.
- The misbalance of the lower back extends to tension and misbalance in the hips and pelvis which can create pressure on the sciatic nerve (where it passes through muscles in the pelvis), pain and strain in the muscles of the hips

and groin, and inflammation and deterioration of the hip joints.

As we continued with Toni's visit, she took us out to her car. It had a firm, flat seat bottom, although the back support somewhat slanted back. As Toni sat down, she positioned her lower back against the back of the seat, and then, as she reached for the wheel, she assumed the same rounded position we had seen in our office. When we guided her head to balance forward and up on top of her spine, Toni's position shifted and she commented that she felt like she was leaning way back. We pointed out that her car seat was slanted back, and now her whole spine was lengthening with the slant of the seat. When her spine was lengthened completely into the same slight slant of the seat, and her head was balancing on top of the spine, even though it felt a bit "stretchy," she also noticed that it took pressure off the painful strain she had been experiencing. Toni was surprised that she was holding no tension in her back, even though it was lengthened out. This demonstrated to her that the spine lengthens when the muscles stop tightening.

Lack of balance and support in the upper spine and neck leads to a lack of balance and support in the lower spine and pelvis. The most problematic result is rounding of the lower back and tucking

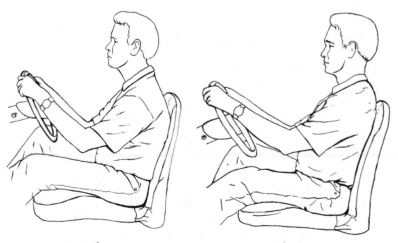

Risk   *Advantage*

inward of the pelvis. In the illustration of Risk, notice the harmful bending forward in the neck, upper and lower back. Notice in the Advantage illustration how the spine is lengthened from top to bottom.

Even with a slanted seat, Toni was able to begin discovering the Advantage that would bring her relief in driving. If you drive in a slanted position, some of your neck muscles need to adjust to balance the head on top of the spine. Commanding your Advantage, you can balance and lengthen your spine.

During the end of Toni's first visit, we taught her the Lying Down Procedure. Toni noticed how she was "melting" back into the floor as she followed our guidance, and that this procedure gave her relief from her pain. We instructed her to use this procedure for twenty minutes each day until her next visit.

As illustrated in Toni's story, doing all you can to change your seat may not take care of the problem. Sitting and driving with your Advantage will enable you to identify the inadequacies in your seat design. In the end, it is not the seat you can depend on to take care of you but rather yourself and how you use your body.

The next step to take in establishing your Advantage is to learn how to lengthen your spine while driving rather than compressing it.

What Is Your Advantage in the Driver's Seat?

After learning to recognize risk and learning the beneficial forward and up coordination of your head and neck, your Advantage will depend on knowing when you are pulling down or acting in a harmful manner. Once your Advantage is established you will feel that these harmful habits are awkward and uncomfortable immediately when they happen. This is healthy Awareness. You want to avoid pulling down with tension, as in the illustration of Risk. And you want to coordinate ease and balance so that your spine really lengthens, as in the Advantage illustration.

On Toni's second visit, we repeated working with the Lying Down Procedure to help her gain maximum release of tension while lengthening and widening throughout her body. Following this, when we observed her in the driver's seat, we could see that she was trying to apply what she had learned in the previous visit about sitting in a slanted position, although with some tension. Then we asked her to place her hands on the wheel and show us her driving position again. As she reached out, we suggested she use the same Directions (words and visualize Primary Control) she had just been using in the Lying Down Procedure, except now to let her back "melt" into the seat back. Immediately she released her tension and her spine lengthened with the slant of the seat. Toni smiled, realizing that the delightful sense of relaxation she felt during the Lying Down Procedure was a quality she could experience while driving.

Procedure for Sitting in the Driver's Seat

Start by sitting as you normally do behind the wheel of your vehicle.

- Place your hands on the steering wheel. Now return them to your lap.
- Pause, and them place them on the wheel again. This Pause allows you to interrupt habit and build your Awareness of how you are using your body.
- Command your Advantage. When you feel your Advantage is fully established, allow your arms to ease up to the wheel. Repeat this process, pausing each time to interrupt habit and Command your Advantage.

As you repeat this procedure, begin to locate the joints involved and become familiar with their healthy movement. The head-neck joint is critically important. As you already know, the head sits on top of the spine at a point that is approximately between your ears.

- Gently rock your head forward and backward on the head-neck joint several times while accurately picturing its location.
- Continue moving your head on this joint until you can feel that only your head is moving. Your neck, aligned with the

rest of your spine, eases back with a slight stretch and moves gently up as the head balances forward. Be sure you are not bending forward from the middle of the neck or protruding the neck forward from its base.

- As the head rocks on the head-neck joint, the back widens to create a total coordination reminiscent of the ease experienced in The Lying Down procedure.

While some of you may be aware of uncontrolled tension in your head-neck relationship, others may not feel tension that is actually occurring. With the help of a camera or a friend, verify what is actually happening with your head, neck and shoulders.

- Sit in a neutral position behind the driver's wheel of your vehicle. This means sit comfortably with absolutely no intent to drive or steer the vehicle. Notice the tone in your neck, from the base of your skull to the top of your shoulders.

- Carefully note the position of your head and neck. Use your growing sixth sense, your kinesthetic sense, to determine the position of your head on top of the head-neck joint. Is it forward or back? Is your chin level, jutting out in front, or tucked down?

- Reach up and place your hands on the steering wheel as if you intend to drive away. Make a note of any change in the tone and position of your neck and head. Does tension increase and the neck move forward?

- Observe calmly how movement and tension in the neck are related to the movement of the arms and hands. Because the automatic response of the neck and head goes unnoticed until you slow down to pay close attention to it, habits of tension can easily come to feel "natural" or "normal."

- Leaving your hands on the steering wheel, apply what you learned in the Lying Down Procedure (chapter 5) to lengthen and widen into the back of the seat. Keep in mind that your whole spine can lengthen with the slant of your seat. Moving your head forward and up helps you accomplish this. To accentuate this movement, apply the Neck Free and the Button Procedures from Chapter 5.

Expanding the Body while Driving

As we continued working with Toni, we had her use some procedures that she could apply while driving to release tension. While Toni sat with her hands on the steering wheel, we asked her to push hard against the wheel. The first time she did this, her head, neck and shoulders tensed forward toward the wheel. We asked her to Pause and then push again, only this time, while Commanding her Advantage with her neck and head pushing away from the wheel. As she did this, she could feel her upper back and neck lengthening and widening. She also noticed that pushing in this way made her arms feel well connected with her back.

We asked her next to push with her legs and feet against the floor, using the same principle. First she Paused to Command her Advantage and then pushed her feet away as if trying to stretch out. At the same time her low and mid-back lengthened and widened back into the seat. She learned to move her lower back in the opposite direction of her heels, allowing the entire pelvis area to lengthen and widen. When she combined these two ways of pushing, with the legs and arms together, her entire back lengthened and widened and her limbs felt a powerful connection with her back.

We asked her to simply Command her Advantage coordination and then gently push and release in a much subtler effort. Toni discovered that the more clearly she commanded her Advantage, the easier and more beneficial the movement that followed was. We encouraged her to use this procedure often on those days when she must be in the car a lot. She discovered that these procedures added comfort to her driving and helped her reduce pain while her injury recovered.

Opposing Arms Procedure to Release Tension

Begin by sitting in the seat of your vehicle and Commanding your Advantage, recalling what you have learned in the previous procedures of this chapter.

- Place your hands on the steering wheel and push against the wheel. Notice what you are doing with your neck and shoulders.
- Do your head and neck move forward toward the steering wheel?
- Do your shoulders tense forward toward the steering wheel?
- Stop pushing. Pause. Push against the wheel again, only this time push your mid-back, upper back and neck against the headrest and seat back, away from your hands as they continue to push on the wheel. Your hands and back are stretching away from each other in opposing directions. At the same time, allow your head to tip forward at the head-neck joint.
- Release this push.
- Push and release two or three more times.
- Now Pause to think and Command your Advantage coordination. Continue to Command your Advantage as you push gently and release.
- Repeat two or three times this sequence of Pause—Command Advantage—and push. Try to accomplish the movement more gently and subtly each time.
- For the final time, simply Pause and Command your Advantage coordination and think the directions of your hands and back easing away from each other, releasing tension.

Opposing Legs Procedure to Release Tension

- Stop pushing with your hands, but leave them on the steering wheel.
- Push your feet into the slant of the floorboard near the gas pedal and brake.

- Do your hips feel tense?
- Is your back tightening forward?
- Release this push and return to just sitting.
- Repeat the push again, but this time as you push with your feet, push your lower back into the back of the seat, away from your feet. You are extending your feet and back in opposite directions. Notice the muscles in the back of your legs doing the pushing. Then release the push and return to just sitting.
- Repeat this push and release two or three times.
- Now, Pause, Command your Advantage coordination and then gently push the feet and low back away from each other. Then release the push.
- Repeat this procedure several times, with a brief push and immediate release. Let each time be easier and gentler.
- Reduce this motion to more of a thought than a movement, visualizing the push and release as your feet and back ease away from each other.

After you feel at ease and successful with both opposing arms and opposing legs procedures, combine them, thinking and visualizing the thought and release.

We have almost all of our students learn to use this procedure. Regardless of how bad the seat in their vehicle might be, this gives the driver or passenger a chance to lengthen and widen their back while driving. Whatever kind of vehicle you find yourself in, use these procedure often.

Moving with Your Advantage while Driving

Simple movements you make while driving can really be a grind on your structure if not performed properly. Looking back to merge in traffic or reaching to change the radio station can either mean repeated trauma or an opportunity to release tension and lengthen your spine. When we asked Toni to reach toward the radio control on the dashboard of her car, she bent forward from the middle of her back, leaving her lower back against the seat back. When we asked her about this, she said that's how she always does it.

The biggest problem that the car seat creates is that people seem reluctant to let their backs move away from the seat back, as they reach for the radio control or turn to look for oncoming traffic. Thus the seat itself creates the illusion that it is designed to support you. True support, however, comes from the structure of your body when you move while seated in your vehicle. This was the discovery Albert the realtor made after his disabling injury. He had been twisting his neck to look before merging, while keeping his back against the seat. And like Toni, he was bending in his neck and upper back when he moved, rather than bending at his hip joint to let the spine follow the movement of the head.

To aid Toni in learning how to move with her Advantage while driving, we had her return to the office with us and sit in the chair again. We asked her to lean as far forward as she could, slide her tailbone all the way back in the chair, then sit up. Although she was still rounding her spine forward slightly, she realized how she could move from her hip joints to let her spine follow the direction in which her head was moving. This meant that her lower back was free to move away from the back of her car seat.

What Toni also discovered was that she had a lot of tension in her hip muscles that prevented the joints from moving easily. She began by learning the exact location of the hip joints and how they can move freely in many directions. During the last part of the session, she did the Lying Down Procedure, placing her full attention on releasing tension in her neck and back to allow her back to lengthen and widen. Immediately the tension in her hips released and she could move them effortlessly. When her attention drifted away from the widening and lengthening of her back, her hips became tight again. Toni realized that the Primary Control also influences the muscle tone in the hips. Her habit of carrying her neck forward stimulated the hips to tighten and low back to round when sitting in her car.

Low back and sciatic problems are partially caused when the leg, pelvis and hip joints are not allowed to move in a natural, correctly located coordination. The consequence is the hip joints tighten and

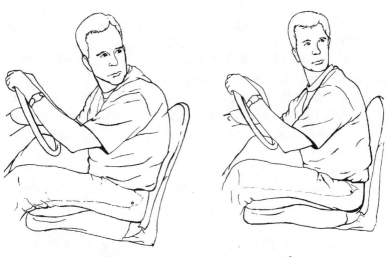

Risk   *Advantage*

restricts the pelvis from moving. Bending then takes place in the lower spine instead of at the hip joints.

The best way to begin establishing your Advantage when moving as you drive is to become aware of your risk:

- Where do you bend in your body as you reach for the radio controls?
- Are your neck and shoulders tense when you turn your head to look before merging in traffic?
- Do you leave your back against the seatback when reaching for the dashboard controls or looking around behind you?
- Do you know if you are "pulling down"?
- Do you turn your head on the head-neck joint at the top of the spine?

Your Advantage depends upon accurately locating and using the following parts of your structure. While sitting in your carseat, do the following simple procedures:

Top of spine:

Locate the joint at the top of your spine, where the head balances. (See page 74) As the head tips forward, notice the back of the head pulling the spine up. Now have the head lead the spine to rock forward in the seat.

Hips:

Refer to page 134 to help you accurately locate your hip joints. Notice in your own body how the leg bone (femur) attaches to the pelvis on the outside. As you rock forward in the seat, notice that the leg bones remain in place while the pelvis moves with the spine to follow the head, easing up as it moves forward.

Spine:

As the head leads forward and up, the spine also moves forward and gently upward.

As you move in your vehicle to look behind you or reach for the radio controls, Pause before moving. Pause interrupts habit and allows you to Command your Advantage. When you have Paused, visualize moving with your Advantage, with the head leading and the spine following upward. The more frequently you interrupt your Risk to visualize your Advantage, the sooner a coordinated and balanced mode of using your body while driving will become automatic. Your goal should be to use the Pause fluently. Pause in action, even if you don't notice any Risk.

Procedure for Reaching Forward and Turning in Your Seat

To do this procedure, as you sit in your car seat, begin by establishing your Advantage: neck free, head releasing forward and up, spine lengthening and widening.

- With your head leading your spine, rock forward at your hip joints as you reach to turn on the radio or put a tape in the tape deck.
- Before you rock back, realize that your head, balanced on top of your spine, still leads upward as you rock back at your hip joint.
- Command your Advantage.

- With your neck free, let your head lead forward and up as you rock forward again. When your spine is vertical or little forward of vertical, locate the head-neck joint at the top of your spine.
- *Maintaining your forward position,* turn your head gently to the left and to the right. Notice how it feels to turn your head at the top of the spine.
- Bring your head back to look straight ahead. Again visualize neck free and allow your head to lead forward and up as you move at your hips to rock back into your seat. Repeat this procedure often to get use to moving to a vertical spine position to reach for controls on the dashboard area and to look around in traffic.

To sum up, the most effective way to establish your Advantage in driving is to:

- Do everything possible to make sure your car seat is not causing problems for your body.
- Learn how to lengthen your spine while driving rather than compressing it.

One of the most dangerous risks in driving is not knowing when you are exerting harmful strains on your body. Repeating the procedures in this chapter many times when you are not in the midst of busy traffic will help reprogram your habits. This will enable your nervous system to respond much more efficiently when you are under pressure and cannot go over each step of the procedure precisely. However, even when you are somewhat distracted, a slight Pause interrupts habit and allows you to once again Command your Advantage. Even though driving can be stressful, driving with your Advantage will help you establish a calm state that enhances your alertness in traffic and increases your comfort.

CHAPTER 8

Reaching and Looking Up

In Chapter 3 on "Early Detection," you met Christine who suffered from shoulder tendinitis working as a hairdresser. Her experiences in learning Alexander Technique were similar to most people we have seen with chronic pain from raising their arms at work. Many people progress in a few visits. At the same time, there are many people who require more time to change.

During the first visit to our office, Christine appeared unsure and anxious to get the appointment over with. She said she was expecting dinner guests and was concerned about being done in time. Her worry mixed with her skepticism that anything would help was reflected in her body's appearance. She was rounding forward with her mid back, shoulders and neck.

We asked Christine to simulate how she stood and used her arms and hands at work. She stood with her knees and hips locked and began to raise her arms, as if she were holding a brush and blow dryer. As she did, her upper back and shoulders rounded further back. Her head and neck protruded forward and her pelvis moved forward even more. It appeared as if she were counterbalancing her arms raised in front by sending her shoulders further back. In this position, her shoulders were left in a strainful disadvantage. We could now see the cause of her shoulder pain. Raising her arms all day with this disadvantage was constantly straining the tendons in her shoulders until they became chronically inflamed.

The risk of injury is not the fact that you must reach out during your job. It is how you use your Primary Control that sets up the injury causing tension.

Who Is at Risk and What Are the Common Injuries?

Assembly workers, painters, hairdressers, hygienists, porters, construction workers, aluminum siding and awning installers, window washers, stockroom and shipping clerks are examples of workers that require looking and/or reaching up. The workers in the above professions are subject to these common varieties of RSI's.

- Tension neck syndrome
- Cervical syndrome
- Thoracic outlet syndrome
- Rotator cuff tendinitis

The risk of injury is not the fact that you must reach out or look up during your job. It is how you use your Primary Control that causes the tension that leads to injury. In this chapter, we will focus on developing your Advantage while reaching and looking up, but will also incorporate movements for lunging and squatting. While your Advantage in these positions is especially helpful for those in occupations requiring them, anyone who reaches and looks up in their daily life can benefit.

Reaching Out and Up

During Christine's visit we asked her to raise and lower her arms several times. The first time she did, we observed her neck and shoulders tightening before her arms and hands moved an inch. Her back and arms then became stiff as she lifted them. We brought this to Christine's attention, and she began recognizing the pattern of strain. She realized that her neck and shoulders began tightening before she started to move her arms, and then further stiffening of the arms, back and legs followed.

When you reach out at work, do you:

- Lock your legs?
- Push your pelvis forward?
- Lean back with your shoulders?
- Tighten your neck and shoulders to begin lifting your arms?
- Keep your arms stiff while you raise them?

If you answered yes to any of these questions, you can begin to recognize the risk that causes injury.

Christine continued to recognize the harmful patterns of tension that were causing her injury. We then progressed to teaching her about her Primary Control and it's Advantage coordination. We explained where the top of the spine really is and guided her head to balance appropriately.

You may want to refresh what you have learned so far about this critical joint.

- Locate the joint at the top of your spine by recalling a mental picture of it being free to move approximately between the ears.
- Visualize your Advantage of your neck free, your head balancing forward and up with your back lengthening and widening.

The next thing we did was help Christine realize why and how she needed to use a Pause to remove risk in raising her arms. We guided her to Pause deliberately before moving to reach in order to release tension in her shoulders and arms. While her arms hung loosely from her shoulders, we had her move in a manner that included her knees and hips flexing with no tension, her lower back moving gently back and her head continuing to balance forward and up. Christine said she felt like an ape in that position, but when she looked at her position in the mirror, she was surprised to see that it looked more upright than when she normally stood. This bending and moving was so slight that she did not appear shorter, rather she gained a fraction of an inch in height. Most importantly,

Christine did not allow the habitual response of tightening her neck and shoulders to begin. We had her move gently from her normal standing balance to this "Monkey" standing balance, so she could watch herself and experience the coordination and become familiar with it.

Learning to bend with the Advantage coordination of lengthening your spine with the appropriate joints moving freely, is the foundation needed to reach up, reach out and reach down. Many teachers of the Alexander Technique and their students, refer to this procedure as "Monkey." When the movement of bending with "Monkey" is used, the spine can lengthen more efficiently than with any other movement.

When you bend to reach for something on the floor, or on your desk, or in a file cabinet, or when you reach up to a shelf, you can eliminate the most risk by integrating "Monkey" into your movement.

Risk   *Advantage*

Releasing up into "Monkey" Procedure

"Releasing up" refers to the coordination of releasing tension in the head, neck and spine relationship (Primary Control) so that the head can ease upward and the spine and body follows it. This is what lengthens the spine. Many people notice an overall sense of lightness when this is accomplished. Trying to push the head up will be accompanied by tension in the spine which can be harmful.

Releasing up can work for you in action while you bend your joints and move with "Monkey," walking or any common daily activity. In "Monkey," the spine and body following the head can continue even when your spine is not vertical, such as continuing to bend with monkey.

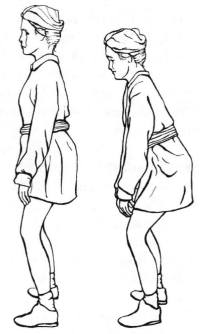

Releasing up into "Monkey"

- Review the directions for standing with your Advantage in Chapter 5.
- Allow your arms to hang loosely at your sides. As your neck releases your head to move forward and up, let your spine release tension and follow your head. This is what we mean by "releasing up." Let this easing upward unweight your legs, then release your knees, hips and ankles so they are free to bend as slightly as possible.
- Let your knees stay balanced over the middle of your feet as they bend.
- As you continue to "release up," let your knees bend again as your lower back moves backward and your head leads the spine forward and up into an inclined position.
- At this point, visualize your Advantage again and let your head lead the spine to lengthen as you stand up.

Repeat this movement again with the emphasis being on "releasing up" as you bend at your hips, knees and ankles. When you achieve a good balance with monkey, your mid and lower back may feel further back in balance than you are accustomed to. This is a natural counterbalancing your body should have. This helps remove the need for the back to strain due to imbalance while bending.

What's going on with your legs?

The more your legs bend with a loose flexibility, the more your back will be free to lengthen and widen.

To aid you in acquiring freedom in your leg joints, exaggerate the beginning of bending with a buckling sensation. You may be surprised how well your legs support you when your joints feel a little wobbly.

Maintain even support in the heels and balls of your feet. As a whole your weight should be evenly distributed between your heels and the balls of your feet.

What about your arms?

During the whole Monkey procedure, your arms should hang loosely from your back and shoulders.

The goal of this procedure is to lengthen and widen your back with this balanced bending coordination, so your arms will move with efficiency and economy.

Tendencies to inhibit or avoid while bending
- bending in the spine instead of hips, knees and ankles
- pulling the head back and down
- squeezing knees together
- tightening legs

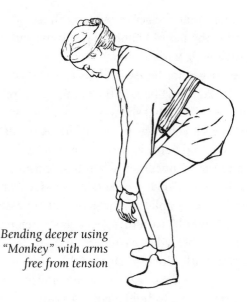

Bending deeper using "Monkey" with arms free from tension

While Christine was maintaining her Advantage with Monkey, we asked her to raise her arms. As she started to raise them, the first thing that happened was the front of her shoulders tightened forward and up toward her neck, and her elbows and wrists stiffened. After she returned her arms to rest at her side, we pointed out that she had been moving her arms as if the joint were in the front collar bone area, and we helped her discover the exact location of her shoulder joint (see illustration on page 96). Again Christine had never dreamed that her arm bone formed a joint with her shoulder blade in the back of the shoulder area.

While she continued to coordinate her Advantage with Monkey, we guided her to let her elbows hang and bend to let her wrists start to rise in front of her. She recognized how her shoulders and neck were not straining as usual. Instead, she felt a sense of comfort and ease. We had Christine move her arms up and down like this several times to become accustomed to it.

Next, we helped Christine learn the Lying Down Procedure. After about ten minutes with this procedure she said that her shoulders felt wonderful, as did the rest of her body. We told her to repeat this everyday for at least twenty minutes. Before Christine left, we recommended that she see how many times per day she could catch herself using her old habitual positions and Pause to coordinate her Advantage with Monkey.

When Christine arrived for her second visit, we asked her how she felt since we last saw her. She said the Lying Down procedure really helped relieve pain and that she was sleeping and waking up without the pain. She said she was unsure of her Advantage with Monkey, however. We told her that it was common for control of the new coordination to be uncertain when first learning it. With that, we reviewed the Lying Down procedure. Christine really loved this part of the work. It accomplished the maximum release of tension throughout her whole structure, especially her neck and shoulder. We found this helped as we moved on to review her Advantage coordination with Monkey. During this visit, we helped Christine learn a greater sense of ease with the movement so that she was not stiffening trying to hold a correct position. After she improved her skill and had a chance to become familiar with it we advanced to the next procedure, The Arm Raising Procedure.

The Arm Raising Procedure

Christine maintained her Advantage with Monkey as she followed our guidance with this procedure. Her neck and shoulders remained free from tension, as her hands moved to contact her collar bones. She then slid her fingers over the top of her shoulders as her elbows raised up to point straight ahead. Christine said she felt no pain, so we had her continue to raise her elbows to a higher angle. Still no pain. Christine was surprised that it did not hurt, as she had learned to expect. We pointed out that she was now using the shoulder joints without the habitual tension. She repeated the procedure with our guidance several times.

Before Christine left, we had her apply the Monkey and new coordinated arm movement to raise her blow dryer and brush. We repeated this with her several times. She felt no pain with it.

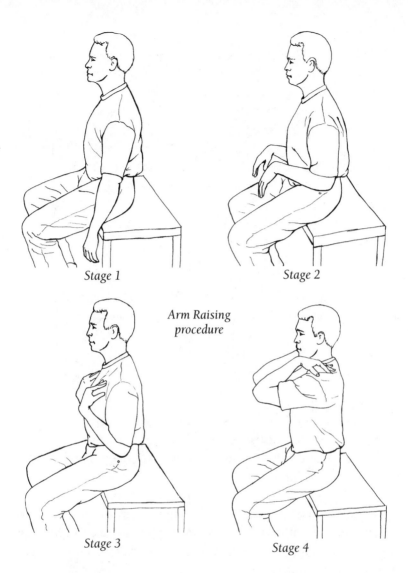

Stage 1

Stage 2

Arm Raising procedure

Stage 3

Stage 4

Raising Your Arms Above You

Recognize risk while reaching up by taking the time to confirm what you do automatically to reach up.

Observe the characteristics of risk in the illustration on the following page.

- The head tightens down as the shoulders tighten up.
- The neck tightens, pulling the head forward.

Risk   *Advantage*

- Stiffness in the shoulders extends down the arms.
- The upper back balances back behind the plumb line.
- The hip and pelvis balance is forward of the plumb line.
- The legs tighten.

Just as important as realizing what aspects of risk are occurring, take time to discover what exactly happens as you first begin to move. Almost without fail, risk starts with the neck tightening causing the shoulders to tense up and somewhat forward to begin the reaching action.

The Importance of Pause

Pause to interrupt the automatic pattern of risk in reaching. While pausing decide to prevent risk as you proceed to reach. Your arms and hands will be the last to move.

When you Pause, take the opportunity to visualize your Advantage.

- Think and visualize your Advantage for "Releasing Up into Monkey."
- Allow the arms to hang from the back and shoulders.
- Move to release up into Monkey.
- To begin moving the arms, let your wrists come up while keeping your attention on Advantage coordination, and allowing the elbows to hang while you inhibit tightening.
- As you bring your hands up higher, let the shoulders and elbows bend loosely.
- Continue to maintain your Advantage of Monkey.
- Let your arms and hands return to hang at your sides with the same loose quality in your joints.

A valuable overview of the progression is:

1) Almost without fail, risk starts with the neck tightening causing the shoulders to tense up and somewhat forward, to begin the reaching action. Start to catch yourself when the unwanted patterns begin.
2) Pause to stop the automatic pattern of risk from taking place, to reach. While pausing decide not to let risk occur when you proceed to reach.
3) The last part of your body to move in reaching is your arms. Move your Primary Control, legs, head and then finally let your arms move.

Hip and Knee Joints

When Christine arrived for her third visit, we asked for a progress report. She had a very pleased look on her face as she told us she had worked without pain and slept very well all week. She was being very religious about applying her Monkey procedure at work, and her level of stress seemed much lower. She commented that bending still felt hard on her legs though, and they got tired easily. As we watched her move with Monkey, we couldn't help but notice tension around her knees and hips. Clearly some work was needed to help her release tightness in these areas. First, we showed her charts illustrating these joints. Then, using our hands, we helped her locate her hip joints and knee joints. After that when she moved with Monkey, a look of surprise and relief came over her face. Her leg joints went from stiff to bending easily.

Hip joint

Locating Hips and Knees

A simple understanding and kinesthetic experience of your hip and knee joints can greatly enhance any activity you need to carry out while on your feet. Start by locating your hip and knee joints and understanding the movement they are capable of.

The hip joints are located on the *sides* of the pelvis. Actually, the bottom of your pelvis is below the height of your hip joints. Many people bend at their waist or low back, instead of using their hip joints. The hip joint is a ball and socket joint which has a wide range of movement, providing you are not restricting it.

Knee joint

The knee joint is located below the knee cap. Most people point at their knee cap when asked to point at their knee joint. The knee bends like a hinge, with the bending taking place below the knee cap. To help realize this more, walk around a little, deliberately thinking about your knees bending at this location.

Hip & Knee Anatomy

Compare these new locations with what you had been doing and continue to recognize the difference in the variety of activities you are involved with daily.

The Lunge

Christine asked a good question at her fourth lesson. She wanted to know how she could use Monkey while shampooing a client. As she demonstrated her customary movements to shampoo, Christine told us "This was how I was taught to shampoo hair in Beauty College." She was used to her feet pointing one way while her body twisted the other way to reach for the person's head in the sink. We taught her the lunge procedure and helped her apply it to the shampoo station. She let one foot step forward with a balanced bend in her knee, with the foot and toes pointing at the sink. She left the other leg and foot extended gently behind her. Christine found it so much easier to reach and work in this position. She commented that she couldn't believe how hard she had been making it on herself.

Lunge Procedure

Using a lunge for bending and reaching is similar to using a one legged Monkey. To prepare for learning this variation for bending to reach, find an open space to move in. Stand with your feet about shoulder width apart.

- With your head leading, allow your right heel to rise up off the floor. This is to help you move your leg with ease.

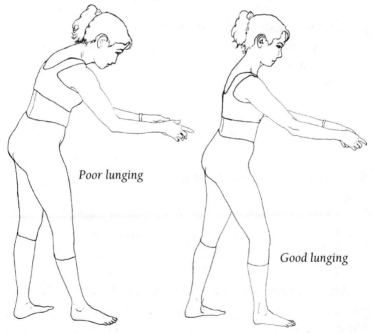

Poor lunging

Good lunging

- Place your right foot in front of you with your toes pointing in the direction you will be bending toward. The back foot may be turned out slightly.
- Maintain your head leading in a forward and up direction as you shift your torso forward at an incline over the front foot.
- Make sure your right knee is bending in line with your big toe and second toe.
- Remind yourself of your basic orders: Neck free, head leading forward and up, spine lengthens and back widens.
- Use your Advantage with the lunge movement to reach.
- To move back to standing let your head lead again to shift your weight backwards so that your weight is distributed between both your legs. Raise your front heel very gently to bring your right leg towards your left as your head leads to return to standing.
- Practice your directions and the movement again. Experiment and try the lunge with your left foot moving forward.

Important points to remember:
- Utilize the ankle, knee and hip joints, not the upper back or mid-back.
- Remember to maintain the poise of your head and the lengthening of your spine in any bending activity.
- When picking objects up, don't let your head pull down towards the objects.

Tendencies to inhibit or avoid while lunging:
- Pulling down toward the object you are lunging for
- Front knee pulling back versus releasing out over toes
- Leading with your face instead of your head forward and up
- Letting your pelvis lead to move forward instead of your head.

Monkey and the Lunge are very appropriate for most situations for bending to reach, pick-up objects and put them away. There are some circumstances where you may be at risk by using them.

- When any object you are holding or picking up is heavy or awkward.
- If you have had a low back injury that has not recovered adequately.

Squatting

In these circumstances, moving with your spine remaining vertical or near vertical will help reduce risk. To accomplish this, use your Advantage coordination with squatting. Squatting is largely acknowledged and taught by many health and safety experts. The important element is the Advantage coordination with Primary Control. This helps lengthen and stabilize the spine. Squatting is also excellent for when you need to use a position to do something on the ground like gardening or working with small children.

We see many people who at first struggle to bend into a squat and find it nearly impossible to maintain balance while continuing to stay in a squatting position. As soon as they succeed in applying the Advantage coordination with their Primary Control, squatting becomes far less difficult.

Risk in Squatting

Misuse with heels down   *Misuse with heels up*

So many people huff and puff, grunt and groan, as they brace themselves to bend into a squatting position. All of this amounts to a lot of tightening which is what really makes the movement so hard. The first risky behavior to recognize in yourself is tightening the neck as you begin to bend. Upon tightening the neck the rest of the spine loses it's lengthening and can easily round backwards putting the lower back at risk. All of this tightening and distortion extends into the hips and knees placing them under excess strain and making it hard for them to move.

Squatting Procedure
With Heels Up
- Begin by standing with your feet approximately shoulder width apart.
- If you feel unsure or unsafe, stand next to a sturdy chair or counter that you can use to steady yourself during movement.
- Command your Advantage.
- Review releasing up the same as you do to begin the movement of Monkey.
- Continue to let your head lead your spine to lengthen in a vertical balance as your knees continue to bend loosely.
- Let your knees bend forward as your heels loosely "pop" up from the ground. You end up on the balls of your feet and toes in a squatted position.
- Continue to have your head moving forward and up during the movement and especially while maintaining the squat.

With Heels Down
Many people find it easier to squat with the heels down. If you are flexible enough, this is a naturally healthy position to use.
- Begin by standing with your feet shoulder width apart or wider. You may want to widen your stance when you squat with your heels down if you feel unstable.
- Command your Advantage.

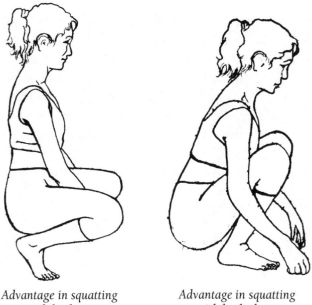

Advantage in squatting with heels up

Advantage in squatting with heels down

- Release up into Monkey. Continue the Monkey so that your spine is continuing an incline.
- Do not let your heels pop up. Let them lengthen into the floor.
- Continue to have your head moving forward and up during the whole movement and especially while maintaining the squat.

Anytime you come up from any squat, let your head lead your spine. Don't let the focus be on your legs. Stay with neck free, head leads and spine follows.

Looking Up

Risk and Awareness:

The first and most important risk to observe and understand while looking up and reaching up is the misbalance of the head, neck and spine relationship. Does your neck bend forward at the base of the neck accompanied by tension and other misbalances in the rest of the spine and legs?

So many people who are at risk or already experiencing pain in their neck and shoulders aren't aware that they can use their spine and head in a different, pain free way. Be certain to verify what is actually happening with your own head, neck and shoulders when you are performing tasks related to looking and reaching up. Despite how you think or feel you are doing, get an accurate image of yourself. Don't trust what feels right or necessary in looking up. The most ideal method is to have a friend video tape you or take photos of you in action. Then watch your video and compare your image to the pictures in this chapter.

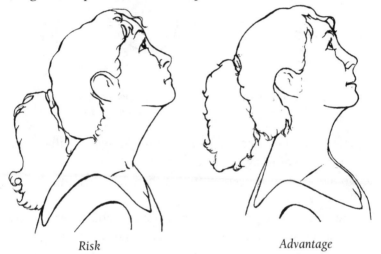

Risk   *Advantage*

The illustration of risk above shows the neck tightening forward. On the other hand, the illustration of Advantage shows the neck lengthening up. Unfortunately, most people unknowingly, put themselves at risk when looking up. These tendencies are associated with tension and pain in the neck, shoulders and upper back.

Repeatedly moving with this risk daily will cause injury. So often, the risk and problems don't stop in the neck and shoulders. Most people who look up as part of their job are doing so while standing. Consequently, the misbalance and tension extends down the rest of the body.

Risk   *Advantage*

Observe the illustrations above. The position of risk imposes a compression on the spine and leg joints. The spine is arching forward with the hips extended too far forward. The knees are locked, creating stiffness and lack of mobility.

Looking Up While Standing

- Be aware of your weight distribution. Is your weight more forward at the balls of your feet? As a whole your weight should be evenly distributed between your heels and the balls of your feet. When the weight is more on the balls of the feet, the pelvis is most likely thrust forward.
- Be sure your hip joints are aligned under your ears.
- Check the joints of your legs. Are the hips, knees and ankles stiffening to stand and reach? Allow a slight flexion to occur in all the joints.

Most Alexander Technique students remark at how unusual it is to stand and look up with a sense of slightly bending in the hips, knees and ankles. It may feel like bending, but if you see yourself on film you will look upright. More importantly:

- You will maintain your plumb line.
- Your arms will be balanced at your sides without tension.
- Your hips, knees and ankles will be free from tension with a quality of loose flexion.

Stopping the Unwanted Risk

Now that you may be recognizing the risk of muscular tension and the relationship of the head and neck, you may be able to identify when it starts. It starts as you intend to look up or reach, before you begin the movement to look up or raise the arms to reach. The neck tightens and moves forward, the head pulls down, and the shoulders tense up.

This is where you must Pause. As you stand with the intent to reach up for an object, decide you are not going to look up and or reach up. The more you interrupt risk, the sooner it will change. The next step is to Look Up with Your Advantage.

When you feel Your Advantage is as complete as possible, do not let your neck go forward.

- First, let your head lead to "release up into monkey."
- Then allow your eyes to lead your head to look up.
- Continue to leave your neck free (not tightening forward).
- Locate the joint at the top of the spine and let your head move there to look up. We tell our students to think of the movement happening at the joint between the ears.

The goal of this procedure is to learn to leave your neck at ease in order to move your head in a balanced Advantage.

Recommended Course of Action with this Chapter

Take this information and apply it to your work activity with the following recommendations. Remember to Pause two or three times each hour during your work day. Do this every day for the first week. If you are successfully pausing this often at the end of this first week, you will be succeeding.

During that Pause, remember to visualize Your Advantage. Keep this simple. Think and picture neck free, head balanced Forward and Up, back lengthen and widen. No matter what you are in the middle of doing, you can visualize your Advantage.

Just before starting your job each day, take a few minutes to organize your Advantage. Move slowly and easily, releasing up into Monkey, and coming back to balanced standing. Then repeat the same Monkey with the reaching procedure, followed by returning to balanced standing.

If you are patient and persistent with these instructions, you will gain the Advantage over stress and risk of injury at your job. Don't be deterred from continuing to practice these Procedures because you may not be perfect in the beginning. Your first step will be paying more attention to your self with awareness and understanding. The more you succeed with that, the easier everything else will follow.

CHAPTER 9

Beyond Recovery & Prevention

Throughout this book we have focused primarily on how Alexander Technique is valuable for overcoming chronic pain and limitations. There is another side to the story, as well. Those who learn Alexander Technique experience a surprisingly positive increase in many areas of their worklife.

Optimal Performance

"In the zone" and "In the bubble" are terms that describe the state of being that performers and athletes achieve when their performance feels effortless and is at its best. Psychologist Abraham Maslow called this "Peak Performance." The traits of Peak Performance are that you feel good both during and after your action, and that it is surprisingly easy and stress-free. Rather than trying hard to do something well, a major part of attention is placed on how the body is being used. This indirect approach frees the potential for clarity in perception, communication, judgment and movement.

F.M. Alexander based his work on his realization that there is no separation between the mind and body. This means not only that your mental and psychological state of mind influence how you feel physically, but also that *how you use your body affects your state of mind.* In helping both himself and other actors and actresses overcome speech problems and improve their theater performances, Alexander demostrated that tension and misbalance in the overall coordination of the body got in the way of performance, production and creativity.

Your own best performance at work, as well as outside of work, will depend on establishing Your Advantage. Using your Advantage to achieve your peak performance will save your mind and body from being worn down and will take you to new levels of performance and creativity, as so many of our clients have discovered.

Increased Productivity

When Sean first came to us, he was nineteen years old and employed at a large insurance company. His job included alternating tasks—sorting mail for one week and processing claims the next week. Sean's injury wasn't work-related; he was recovering from a car accident. But the pain in his neck and loss of power in his arms was affecting his performance at work. Despite this, he had a very upbeat attitude and was determined to return to complete health and to his participation in athletics again.

As Sean started learning Alexander Technique, he discovered how much he tightened his neck by pulling his head down to complete such simple tasks as bending over to pick up a pencil. Of course the excessive tension in his neck was extending to his back and into his arms. As he learned to apply his Advantage, he not only recovered strength in his arms, but he was also surprised to see how much less effort it took for him to move when he was not tightening his neck. This translated into unexpected success at work.

Sorting mail was a pressured aspect of Sean's job that included a time and quota demand. Even though his new coordination felt strange, Sean managed to maintain awareness of the balance of his head and neck while doing this task. Without intending to, he surpassed his quota considerably and earned praise from his supervisors for attitude and performance. Sean attributed this to using what he had learned from Alexander Technique.

The bottom line at most jobs is to work efficiently. Efficiency is a combination of speed, accuracy and endurance, all of which are enhanced by moving without tension and in balance. Working with your Advantage is sure to increase your own efficiency while bringing you relief from tension.

Reduced Stress

Paula is a high ranking officer in a major metropolitan police department. At fifty years of age, Paula has had a full career as a police officer. She came to Alexander Technique because of stress-related pain, attributed to her job. Her work often meant confrontations with criminals as well as with male police officers who were her colleagues. Her pain was focused in her upper back and shoulders, and the stress in her face was obvious.

Paula discovered through Alexander Technique how she was holding her neck and shoulders with excess tension, which was a physiological response to stressful stimuli. This reaction of tension had become a constant in all her actions. We worked together on reducing the tension in her first session. When Paula arrived at her second session, one week later, looking very at ease, I commented on her appearance and asked if she had experienced an easy day. She answered "No," and went on to tell us that, in fact, she had just come from a major confrontation with her superior officer. She said she had remained aware of how her neck and shoulders had wanted to tighten while he was talking to her but that she had managed to Pause and inhibit that tension during most of the exchange. While it seemed to Paula that she said and did very little during the conversation, it ended with her superior conceding to her perception.

For Paula, learning Alexander Technique not only meant rapidly recovering from her stress-related pain, but also learning to stop tightening in reaction to stress. No longer a victim of her own reactions, she felt more in control of situations at work and at home.

No environment can be entirely stress-free or perfectly ideal, but by becoming fluent with your Pause and coordination of your Advantage, you can learn to choose your responses to stimuli in the environment rather than be a victim of them. In this way, you can learn to adapt to the increased pace of change and excel in a changing environment.

Not only does your ability to minimize your stress have a positive effect on you, it has a beneficial effect on others around you as well. Gay has taught primary school for seven years. Before she came to us to learn Alexander Technique, Gay had tried chiropractic treatment, physical therapy and massage to relieve the pain in her shoulders and neck that would escalate most school days into a headache. She found that keeping her attention on 25 children all day and responding appropriately to each was stressful. But when she was stressed, she could see that the children picked up on it and reacted in an unruly manner.

As we helped to release the tension in her neck and bring her head into balance, her overall tension was relieved. Like many others learning Alexander Technique, Gay could see how to release tension in that moment with us, but she couldn't imagine being able to use the method while meeting the challenge at work. In her case, the work challenge was being in charge of a classroom full of children. How could she be aware of her students and think about how she was using her body at the same time?

In Chapter 4, you were introduced to the two fields of awareness we function in simultaneously. One field of awareness is your environment and the task you are performing. The other field of awareness is inside yourself, knowing what you are doing with your body and mind and how you are doing it. What Gay discovered through Alexander Technique is that these two seemingly separate fields of awareness are actually connected.

At the end of her first four weeks with us, Gay was experiencing far fewer days of tension and pain per week but she reported that she was still rarely able to use her Advantage, especially when her class became hectic and stressful. We encouraged her to trust that putting more attention on herself would actually lower the level of hectic stress in her job. The following day she had an enlightening experience. When her class started to get chaotic, she observed her reaction and paused to command her Advantage. As soon as she stopped her stressful response, to her surprise the children calmed down.

Gay wanted to know what accounted for this. First, we told her, in stopping her stressful response, Gay could see, hear and feel her environment differently—she could see the whole picture, not only the problems. Secondly, when the teacher no longer felt stressed, a stressful stimulus for the children was removed. After six weeks of Alexander Technique, Gay reported that whereas her previous reaction had seemed to act as a blinder, allowing her to focus only on what was stressful, she now felt that her awareness of the class was expanded, and she could more easily perceive the class in its entirety.

This sense of opening and ease is another aspect of what establishing your Advantage can bring into your work and your life.

Enhanced Creativity

While Darlene, like most of our clients, came in for relief from pain, she ended up experiencing what Peak Performance means. Darlene is an analyst with the state government, responsible for producing reports for publication. The majority of her work time is spent at a computer and in meetings, and she is continually under pressure. The pain in her head, neck and shoulders, which started with an auto accident, had been getting worse at work. I noticed that she appeared to be holding her head and neck "in traction," as if she did not want to disturb their position. As she learned to stop the tightening and to move and carry out her daily activities with the poised balance of her head and neck, she managed to recover from the injury. But it was the unexpected side effects that Darlene was most thrilled about.

With a deadline to meet on an important report, Darlene had gone into work on a Saturday. As she sat in front of her computer screen, she came down with a bad case of writers' block. In an instant, she recognized the dreaded pattern of pain and tension in her head, neck and shoulders. At that point Darlene applied what she had been learning in Alexander Technique, stopped thinking about the report she was responsible for, and started thinking about her Advantage. Using some of the procedures in this book, she started Commanding her Advantage while sitting at her desk. Next she let her arms hang easily, letting her elbows move freely as she raised her wrists up and down. Then she added a loose rotation of her wrists. She started to apply these movements to typing on her keyboard. Before she knew it, her pain had gone away and ideas for the report started pouring out. In the midst of meeting a critical deadline, Darlene found that she was feeling playful as she worked. She almost felt guilty that it didn't feel like "working," yet she produced a great report.

When you inhibit the so-called physical response of tension, your mental and psychological capacities are freed up and creativity can flourish.

Improved Public Speaking

The success of many professionals depends on their ability to communicate well and to speak in public. The ability to do so is linked with the ability to remain relaxed under pressure. Stan is an attorney who regularly attends cases in the courtroom. One day, after witnessing a colleague in complete command of the courtroom, Stan's dissatisfaction with his own speaking performance came to a head. Impressed with the other lawyer's poise, he approached him after the court session to ask him about his superior performance.

The other attorney told him that he was using skills he had learned from Alexander Technique.

When Stan came to his first session, he told us that he felt his voice was weak and choppy. He said he would usually have to strain to think about what he was saying and wondered how the judge and jury were responding to him. At the end of a day in court he would feel fatigued and burnt out. Stan spent ten weeks learning Alexander Technique before he actually made a personal commitment to use it in a courtroom situation. What he found was that, in contrast to his previous performances, he felt relaxed and easily monitored the responses of the judge, jury and appellate court representative. He said his voice was resonant and under control, and he felt as if he was saying less but was clearer in his speaking. At the end of that day Stan felt great. For him Alexander Technique had nothing to do with recovery from or prevention of injury but with learning how to get "in the zone" and use his full abilities in his profession.

As you become fluent with your Advantage coordination, the lack of tension will allow your body to operate without strain and increase your speed and alertness. At times you may feel very light or as if you are doing next to nothing. Working with your Advantage is always a positive experience. Tension is no longer sapping your energy, and you will no longer experience the mental blocks associated with too much stress. Learning how to inhibit tense reactions by establishing your Advantage will lead to your own Peak Performance at work and throughout the activities of your life.

APPENDIX A

Training Solutions

If you are a business owner or manager, you know how important it is for you and your employees to remain healthy and productive. The Advantage Training, offered by the Pacific Institute for the Alexander Technique, is specially designed to address the needs of businesses in:

- Understanding and preventing Repetitive Strain Injuries
- Recovering from Repetitive Strain Injuries
- Promoting optimal performance in your employees

The Advantage Training includes both hands-on and verbal instruction to introduce your work force to consciously controlling physical stress and understanding the key to optimal performance. In the course of the training, your employees will learn to work with greater ease and efficiency as well as to avoid some of the most basic causes of Repetitive Strain Injuries and stress-related diseases.

As we make clear in *Working Without Pain*, only so much can be changed in the working environment to prevent Repetitive Strain Injuries. The rest depends upon skillful use of the body in action. The training staff from The Advantage Training have been teaching clients how to correct various strain and stress-related disorders since 1977. At our locations and at doctors' offices, we have helped hundreds of people reorganize how they use their bodies in order to overcome and prevent work-related pain in the hands, arms, shoulders, back and neck .

In offering the Advantage Training to your employees, you can choose from three formats:
1) Lectures and Presentations
2) The RSI Prevention Training
3) Customized Training and Materials

OPTION #1: Lectures and Presentations

We adapt our presentations to make them relevant to the specific patterns of strain encountered by the audience. Simple experiential techniques convey to those present the relaxed and alert quality available to them as they work with the Advantage Training. The following topics are covered in the format of lectures which includes demonstrations of various procedures based on the Alexander Technique.
- The Hidden Causes of Repetitive Strain Injuries
- The Keys to Stopping Repetitive Strain Injuries
- Mastering Optimal Performance

OPTION #2: The RSI Prevention Training

The RSI Prevention Training is geared toward producing a significant level of change in your work force. Presented on-site in your place of business, the training takes place over a period of consecutive weeks and consists of three phases:

Phase One: Emphasis on individual instruction with small group support. To establish the momentum of change, each student is observed and instructed at their workstation. Small group meetings for further instruction provide a context for mutual support. During this phase the basics of Alexander Technique are presented, and visual aids such as videotaping participants may be utilized.

Phase Two: Emphasis on group instruction with support from private work. Instruction includes inhibiting harmful patterns and reinforcing the application of the Advantage to job-specific situations.

Phase Three: Whole group instruction. In this final phase, participants will receive individual support as necessary, but the emphasis remains on the group as a whole putting their Advantage into action.

We have found in our work with organizations that to guarantee long-lasting results, it is essential that the entire program be carried out. Just as antibiotics are effective when taken for their fully prescribed course, our program requires a complete course of instruction.

OPTION #3: Customized Training and Materials

To aid you and your employees in preventing Repetitive Strain Injuries and promoting optimal performance, we can work with you to create customized guidebooks and audio/video tapes. Your company can have manuals and audio visual materials prepared by The Advantage Training.

You may want to schedule your first Advantage Training with your highest risk workers. The results will be pleasing and inspiring to everyone in your company. The cost of our program actually constitutes a savings compared to the cost of unaddressed problems that can lead to Repetitive Strain Injuries and the loss of work time and medical expenses that follow in their wake. In addition, the Advantage Training is an investment in the performance and well-being of you and your employees.

The Advantage Training is a subsidiary of The Pacific Institute for the Alexander Technique (PIAT), which has been licensed with the California Department of Education since 1985 and is approved by the North American Society of Teachers of the Alexander Technique, (NASTAT) to train teachers. NASTAT is recognized internationally as an organization of qualified Alexander Technique teachers. NASTAT, 3010 Hennepin Ave. South, Suite 10, Minneapolis, MN.

The work of PIAT includes:

- The Advantage Training and lecture/presentations for businesses and organizations on prevention of and recovery from RSI's and developing optimal performance in the workplace.
- The Alexander Technique Teacher training program. Students complete a full-time, three year training to gain the skills of a qualified teacher of the Alexander Technique.

The Pacific Institute is one of two training programs in the United States that have approval by the Immigration and Nationalization Service to accept foreign students.

- Private practice. Instruction is offered individually and in small groups to assist clients with a wide range of needs.
- Publishing. Books, audio and visual learning aids to teach the Alexander Technique are produced by members of our staff.
- Product Distribution. We sell selected quality products, such as specially designed seat cushions, that are affordable solutions to enhance your environment.

For more information on *The Advantage Training* and the Alexander Technique, call Bruce Oliver or Sherry Berjeron-Oliver at (916) 894-7166 or toll free at (800) 860-1200—at the voice prompt, enter 239403.

E-mail: piat@sunset.net

Write to us at:

The Advantage Training
1530 Humboldt, #4
Chico, CA 95928

APPENDIX B

Product Solutions

How much time do you spend sitting down? In your office, in your car, at conferences, on airplanes? Do the seats you spend long hours sitting in provide adequate support for your Advantage? Chances are that they not only lack support but may even be hurting you. Because good office chairs and car seats are usually costly, most people make the most out of what they have. However, there are some inexpensive solutions for enhancing any seat you use—well-designed and affordable cushions that support a healthy balance in your Primary Control. If you are encountering any of the following problems, your solution is readily found in our portable and adjustable seat cushions.

Common Problems

In the Office: You may find that your office chair is too deep from front to back—or too shallow. Perhaps your feet don't touch the floor, or you have to lean back too far in order to have the support of the seat back. If the seat bottom is worn out, or the chair is not adjustable, you may be experiencing stress that over time can culminate in Repetitive Strain Injuries. Even your ergonomically-designed chair may not "fit" adequately. Yet good and durable office chairs are usually very costly. Self-employed people often have difficulty justifying the cost of buying one for their own use. For small businesses, buying good chairs for all employees may just not be within the budget.

Traveling in Vehicles: Auto and truck seats are notoriously inadequate for a healthy Primary Control. They are poorly designed and wear out quickly. The result is that your sit-bones and spine may lack support. Drivers and passengers have no surface sufficient for lengthening, widening and supporting their backs. Chronic low back pain and sciatica may result. Neither do the contours of bucket seats encourage the spine to lengthen, and they may be positioned too low to see clearly in traffic. Hours spent in airplane seats, which often compress the spine, can also stress your back.

At Conferences: We often see in our clients that the days following a conference are a time of misbalance and pain in the body. We call it "Chair Trauma." In many conferences, participants sit for most of the day listening to speakers and presentations. Often the chairs they are using are folding chairs or those made of molded plastic. When the back rest on a chair slants backwards considerably, your neck must work harder to keep your head balancing on top of the spine. When the chair bottom inclines back, your legs are forced into an upward slant from your hips to your knees, which places serious strain on your back. Molded plastic chairs are rounded at the point where your lower spine meets the back of the chair. This lack of support is particularly stressful for your lower back and legs.

The Solutions

Seat Back Cushion (Item #A11)

The Seat Back Cushion works to improve your chair or car seat in two principle ways:

1) It creates a firm, flat surface against which your spine can lengthen and widen, similar to what you experience lying down in the Semi-Supine Position.

2) It reduces the backward incline of your chair or car seat, thereby supporting your neck in maintaining the head balanced on top of the spine.

For those with chronic low back problems, the necessary additional support for the lumbar curve is provided by the adjustable lumbar cushion that comes with this cushion. It easily adjusts to fit your back, giving extra support where you need it. It may also be easily removed if you do not need it.

Extra Thick Seat Back Cushion (Item #A12)

The Extra Thick Seat Back Cushion creates a back surface that scoots you closer to the front of your chair, or closer to the steering wheel, while providing a beneficial surface for your back. Like Item #A11 this Seat Back Cushion comes with an adjustable lumbar cushion. The lumbar cushion easily adjusts to fit your back, giving extra support where you need it, and it may be easily removed if you do not need it.

Seat Bottom Cushions (Item #A13)

To counteract the harmful backward slant of poor seat bottoms, the slightly wedge-shaped Seat Bottom Cushion provides extra support under your sit-bones and tapers down in front .

All of the cushions are designed to be complimentary to your Advantage. They are firm with a forgiving softness. They have been tested by people of many different sizes and shapes. The fabric is a handsome tough wearing and breathable material. Everything is manufactured in the United States of America.

The people using them report how much comfort the cushions add to sitting and how much better they feel after sitting for long periods. These cushions are being put to use at computer work stations, in airline seats, in automobiles and at conferences-all locations where people normally experience difficulty and pain.

These cushions combined with your Advantage coordination and Awareness will protect you from the Repetitive Strain Injury resulting from "chair trauma."

To purchase any of these cushions, fill out the Order Form on the following page.

Seat Cushion Order Form

To order any of the products, complete this form and send it with check or money order to:

PIAT
1530 Humboldt Rd., #4
Chico, CA 95928
or call (916) 894-7166 and use your Visa Card or Mastercard

QTY.	ITEM#	DESCRIPTION	PRICE	AMOUNT
_____	A11	Back cushion with adjustable lumbar support	$32.95ea.	_____
_____	A12	Extra thick back cushion with adjustable lumbar support	$32.95ea.	_____
_____	A13	Bottom cushion	$32.95ea.	_____

State Tax (Calif. only) 7.25% _____

Shipping & Handling* _____

*Shipping and handling charges: 1-4 cushions: $ 4.00
5-10 cushions $ 6.00

TOTAL _____

Name: _____

Organization: _____

Address: _____

City, St, Zip: _____

Phone: _____

Fax: _____

E-mail: _____